Working with 1

C000241568

SHAMANIC

Working with Tree Spirits in

SHAMANIC HEALING

Peter Aziz

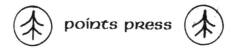
points press

PUBLISHED BY POINTS PRESS
PO BOX 90, TOTNES, DEVON TQ11 0YG

ISBN 0-9524358-0-2

Cover Design by Glennie Kindred

First Published 1994

Printed in Great Britain by
Antony Rowe Ltd.
Chippenham, Wiltshire

CONTENTS

Contents

Contents

Contents

LIST OF ILLUSTRATIONS

TABLES

INTRODUCTION

Healing and initiation are truly one process. All sickness is caused by the illusions we hold, so healing can be seen as a gradual awakening to reality. But what is it that allows us to shed our illusions? It is unconditional love, as expressed by Nature. Nature alone is free of conditioning. From birth we are conditioned by the human world and all kinds of limitations are forced on us. When we leave the human world and return to Nature, these limitations can begin to fall away because our souls have a chance to see pure creation without anybody around to manipulate our attitudes. It is then that we discover a love so strong and which resonates so closely with our innermost souls that the bondage of human conditioning has no hope of holding us. It has been said in the Chaldean scrolls that the foolish man looks upon Nature and sees darkness, but the wise man looks upon the face of Nature and beholds the luminous countenance of the Eternal. Nature is a perfect mirror of our souls. What we see in Nature depends upon how willing we are to see ourselves.

The purity and freshness of the energy Nature gives to us cannot be found elsewhere. If you observe the abundance Nature gives so freely, to every creature, without judgement, you truly see unconditional love in action. Trees drop all their fruit, withholding nothing, and do not judge whether someone is worthy or not to receive their fruit. Likewise, the sun, the air, and all things of real value are freely available to all. Nature is truly the purest expression of our creator; it is in Her that the Shaman seeks power. And to carry that power to others is to heal. When the glory of that love works through you, others must shed their conditioning and find beauty and strength. Love truly heals far better than any of the techniques invented by human minds. Notice how masters such as Jesus healed by presence alone, without the use of any techniques. It is the strength and purity of the soul shining through which causes a patient to awaken from illusion and thus brings about healing from within.

So few know what love truly is. You cannot heal with an

outpouring of emotion or sentimentality. Love is measured by how much we are willing to give to a cause beyond ourselves. If we are not willing to work to help someone, how can we say then that we love? Knowing that healing comes from love is not an excuse for not studying hard. If someone you truly love is ill, wouldn't you make every effort to learn how to give them the best possible treatment? Love is developed by applying it through work. Nobody ever grows through selfishness. When we open ourselves to the great love expressed by Nature, and then let it manifest through us by giving our best, sometimes with great sacrifice, it is then that we truly grow.

Learning this type of work is not an intellectual process. In modern society, the intellect is over-used, at the expense of other faculties. It should be clear, however, that the mind cannot grasp as much as our deeper feelings. If you think about the way in which the Sun sees only half way round the world, whilst the affect of the Moon and its control over the waters reaches round the whole world at all times, you will understand that similarly our lunar side, the side of our deepest feelings, grasps far more than our intellectual minds. Most people have closed themselves to that greater part of reality which is only accessible to the feelings, and yet it is these hidden forces that control and shape their lives.

It is the task of the Shaman, therefore, to open to this greater reality, and use feelings to the full. To do this you must have an interest in what you wish to feel, and the amount of interest you have for other beings depends upon the amount of love you have. So love is again the key. And the seed of love within us grows through our connectedness with Nature.

The purpose of this book is, firstly, to give you a sense of how inner reality works through our lives, and creates our health as well as our physical environment, and secondly, to describe healing techniques. These healing techniques are examples of how a Shaman uses knowledge of this reality to bring about healing on many levels. The techniques contain, most importantly, meditations and exercises with Nature, which will help you make a direct contact with the source of truth within.

Introduction

As you grow, through using these exercises, you need to be aware that your mind may react in ways which seek to pull you off your path. Your subconscious has found a nice safe perception of reality, and does not wish to be threatened by a different view of reality. It will produce all kinds of red herrings to prevent you from discovering that greater reality. These may manifest as emotional reactions, mental arguments or situations which make it difficult for you to carry on. To get over these resistances, it is important to stop and observe your reactions, rather than allow them to carry you away, and to keep your will focused on your task. Perform the exercises diligently, and be constantly aware of your desire to expand into a greater reality.

At times, as you face many of your resistances, it may seem like hard work, but you will discover that the power that wishes you to succeed is far greater than that which seeks to restrain you. As you let go of the need to grasp everything with the mind, and open to the deeper wonders of Nature from your heart, you will find that power is born of joy!

I

FUNDAMENTAL PRINCIPLES

There are certain principles that keep us at one with our creator, and all illness comes from a deviation from these principles. In order to understand these fundamental principles, the Shaman learns by observing the ways of the soul, and how life and health are created. This approach is different to that of medical science, which studies sickness rather than life. Medical science limits the study of life to the physical body. But when you dissect the least creature, you are left with a corpse, and the connection with the soul is lost. This form of science is of no value to us.

I sometimes use the terminology of medical science to explain to a modern mind how shamanic healing works, and sometimes it is necessary to clothe truth in words that make it more acceptable, but, it is only the application of shamanic principles that brings about true healing.

The first principle is *honouring our originality*. Originality is the quality that most closely reflects the spark within. When we give up our own ideas, perceptions and visions, to follow what others insist is right, we deny our innermost truth. This leads to resentment for not having fulfilled our true purpose, and a need to judge everything else.

This brings us to the next important principle; *non-judgement and acceptance*. When we judge we deny one half of a duality, and, therefore, deny a part of ourselves. When we are unable to accept any experience, we begin to build up negative emotions. Often we also judge ourselves for having these emotions and, therefore, suppress them. It is becoming increasingly well known that suppressed emotions damage our physical bodies.

The next important principle is to approach life with *unconditional love* or *enthusiasm*. It is this that enables us to transmute the negative emotions we hold. We suppress experiences through our unwillingness to lovingly endure them, because there is not enough love or enthusiasm to allow us to accept the situation. When we are filled with love, with no conditions on love, we are able to encompass all our pains and frustrations.

The next principle is *self-responsibility*. This is the recognition that we create our own reality, and that our lives are perfect manifestations of our inner consciousness. Everything that ever happened in our lives, we created ourselves. All those who happen to be involved in our traumas and life lessons are just actors, playing their roles in the dance that we ourselves have choreographed. When you realise that you have created everything yourself the need to resent others disappears.

People may spend years trying to clear negative emotions, but as long as the illusion of being a victim remains, they will continue to experience them. For example, imagine that a tool you use daily suddenly goes missing, and you believe that a certain person has stolen it. Every time you need that tool and it is not there, you will resent that person, no matter how many times you forgive him. You may spend months releasing your anger and forgiving him, but each time you need that tool, you will resent him again. Now, supposing you realise that he had not stolen the tool, but instead you have misplaced it. Then there is no more resentment, and no more need to forgive. This is how all life works. We go beyond negative feelings by realising that we are responsible for what we create in our lives. Now this brings us to the issue of forgiveness. Many healers try to work with forgiveness, but if you understand these principles you will see that forgiveness has no place in healing, because in order to forgive, you must first be a victim. If you take responsibility for what you have created, then the need to forgive somebody else does not arise. Often, the need to forgive is born out of judgement, because we are told not to hold negative feelings. In truth, we should accept all our feelings unconditionally.

Fundamental Principles

The next important principle in healing is *discipline*. This means diligently applying the things you know to be true, in spite of the entreaties of your lower nature which would like to lead you in the opposite direction. Your reactive patterns will always seek to maintain themselves, and so it is easier to hold on to old habits of thought and action, rather than to change and grow. It is easier to project your problems onto another person, rather than be responsible for yourself; it is easier to wallow in your feelings rather than lovingly endure them, and it is easier to stick to bad eating habits rather than change to a healthier diet.

Eating properly is another main principle. Diet is important, not only for physical health but for spiritual growth as well. Poor diet helps us to suppress our feelings and, therefore, our consciousness, by clogging the intercellular spaces with mucoprotein, and thereby preventing access to the cellular level of memory. Whenever a person is drawn towards unhealthy food, far from following his true desires, he is simply following the call of his reactive patterns which seek to control him. If you wish to grow or receive any healing, it is first your responsibility to be of sound nutrition.

There are many different ideas about nutrition, but if we are to trust in Nature rather than the minds of men, we must rely on fresh, raw, organic foods. Cooking foods destroys valuable enzymes. Vitamin pills can never replace natural sources; most of the content is a laboratory preparation. You simply cannot fit enough nutrition into the size of pill. These laboratory vitamins act by suppressing symptoms, much like a drug, rather than giving real benefit. It has been proven time and time again that these supplements suppress the natural healing crisis, and therefore block any transformation. Avoid vitamin pills like the plague.

The only real nutrition is provided by Nature without interference from man, i.e. fresh, raw, organically grown fruit and vegetables. One should be prepared to cut down on cooked food, and certainly avoid any refined foods and chemical additives. Diet can be seen as the first step of discipline. It requires just as much diligence to apply the other principles already mentioned.

3

In order to understand how these principles can be applied in healing, we need to understand the reverse, i.e. how ignorance of these principles creates disease. When a person is not exposed to enough of Nature e.g. sunlight, pure food, fresh air, bird song and other natural sound, the pineal gland atrophies and there is not enough enthusiasm to handle life's difficulties. When one experiences pain and cannot lovingly endure it, that pain is suppressed into the pituitary gland.

The person may get angry, and because he or she cannot change the situation, the anger is suppressed, and stored in the thyroid. Then the person fears more pain, and the fear is suppressed into the thymus. Having all these feelings that he or she does not want to face, the person begins to feel like a victim, and he or she is filled with grief. This grief is stored in the adrenal gland. When it is all too much, the person gives up, and the apathy, failure patterns and death wishes which result are stored in the spleen.

Then the person may find some way of closing the feelings away all together, so they do not have to be faced. It may be just an emotional 'blacking out', or, drugs, alcohol, hypnosis or anaesthetics may be involved. All these cause areas of unconsciousness which are stored in the Gonads. The glandular system has reflex actions to all other organs of the body, which, as a result, also degenerate. To finally suppress everything a person's diet changes. He or she is drawn to mucous forming foods, to be sure the cellular memory is inaccessible.

When we correct our diets, we open the door for these feelings to emerge again. We must then be able to accept, lovingly endure and take responsibility for each feeling before we can move onto the next one, so we move up the scale through unconsciousness, apathy, grief, fear, anger and pain, until our consciousness, as well as our body, is cleared.

Accepting negative emotions is something we are often conditioned against, so we need to understand their value. All these feelings are important for our growth. Often, it is fear, intolerance or disappointment that causes us to make necessary changes in our lives. Without these emotions we are likely to remain in an environment which leads to stagnation. When we are disappointed, we have to find something more trustworthy to rely on, and that is an improvement. Emotions only become a problem if they are not used in the right place. Let us take anger as an example. Sometimes we need aggression to stand up for ourselves. If we give in and accept something that is not right for us, we hold on to resentment, become bitter and therefore less loving with others. The anger is not truly stopped, it simply gets directed at the wrong people. How much better life would be if we expressed that anger where it was needed! When any emotions arise, do not judge them, for they have their purpose, but feel them enthusiastically!

There is one emotion that is more conditioned than real, and that is guilt. Sometimes guilt can be real, because you have acted unfairly with others, and in order to progress you will have to make amends so that your conscience does not hold you back, but the majority of guilt stems from false religious conditioning. People are made to feel guilty for enjoying things which have harmed nobody, and this guilt makes them feel unworthy of love or anything else they need, and undermines their self worth. It is impossible to move forward until these guilt feelings are eradicated.

The reason these religious falsities gain such a deep hold, is because the subconscious mind pays much attention to both the written word and figures of authority. To loosen the grip of this conditioning, we need to have a written philosophy that can be recognised as far more reasonable and true.

Read the following over and over again, until the subconscious accepts it and sheds its harmful moral or religious conditioning.

1   *Higher beings must be beyond insult by us, so it is impossible to offend, or sin against, a higher being, or God. We can only offend other lower beings.*

2   *Anything that does not harm another being is not a sin.*

3   *Sometimes we must feel pain in order for the right thing to be done for the highest good of all. That pain is a lesson for us, teaching us to grow out of a useless condition. The pain is not a sin or a punishment.*

4   *Since people manifest their own pain for their own growth, we are not truly responsible for them. We cannot truly sin against others, only against self. We, therefore, require nobody's forgiveness but our own. Our only responsibility is to honour our highest truths.*

5   *Nobody is expected to be perfect, only our creator is perfect.*

6   *All beings deserve love, in spite of their imperfections.*

7   *We are expected to make mistakes in order to realise our imperfections, so that we may surrender to something greater than self. Realising our weaknesses, we can grow, and this is to be praised. It is when we make mistakes that we most need love.*

8   *Nature is oversupplying and wasteful in her abundance. Nature's way is abundance, not lack.*

9   *Nature gives to all, there are none who are undeserving.*

10   *We have been given our various senses to experience and enjoy life to the full. Enjoyment of sensory experience is therefore in perfect harmony with our evolution.*

Your first responsibility is to apply these principles to yourself, they cannot be forced upon another. If you wish to change another person, you must be judging them, and that is not unconditional love. At the same time, you need to make allowances for all the people who will want to change you, or tell you what to do. People will always try and tell you your path, because they have not found their own. You need to be on guard against others, for it is your divine right to follow the dictates of your own conscience, and find your own path. But do not resent others for trying to change you, they are simply lost. Discovering truth even to a small degree separates you from the masses and puts you in a position of responsibility. Become strong and tolerant through your own path, then you can inspire others.

II

SHAMANIC PHYSIOLOGY

As above, so below. Our bodies are a perfect reflection of our inner consciousness. Each organ, gland or part of the body reflects a different aspect of the psyche and when a part of the body is diseased or damaged, that damage stems from a suppression of consciousness or a denial of some aspect of consciousness.

In order to heal any organ it is necessary for the patient to lovingly and willingly endure whatever emotions, memories or thought patterns are stored in that organ. No physical healing method can bring about a permanent cure unless the consciousness is also changed. Furthermore, surgical removal of any organ does not remove its patterns from the consciousness of the individual, since the pattern is reflected in every single cell in the body.

The body is like a three-dimensional hologram, where every cell stores information about the whole body. In the cell the seven turns of the DNA spiral reflect the seven endocrine glands and the seven corresponding levels of suppressed emotion (see Chapter 1). The organs of the body reflect the activities of the glands and, therefore, will store similar patterns.

A particular pattern of consciousness is symbolic of the function performed by the organ or gland which stores it. The next sections provide a guide to these inner meanings of the glandular system and the major organs of the body.

The Glandular System

Pineal Gland

This is the master gland that controls the functions of all the other glands. Its healthy function depends upon enthusiasm, and it requires natural sunlight. When there is not enough enthusiasm flowing in from Nature, consciousness begins to suppress experience, and then the other glands, in turn, suppress all the different emotions.

Pituitary Gland

This stores suppressed pain. It can also be seen as a master gland which controls the other five, lower, glands. Experiencing the pain that has been stored in this gland can be a doorway to higher consciousness, after the suppressions and judgements of the lower glands have been transmuted. Judgements are formed on this level. Lovingly enduring pain allows the encompassing of dualities and the release of judgment.

Thyroid Gland

This stores anger. Anger causes a person to desire power and results in a rigid attitude. When the thyroid does not function normally, the normal process of calcification in the bones and joints goes awry, resulting in arthritis or rheumatism. It can be seen that a rigid body stems from a rigid mind.

Thymus Gland

This stores fear, and governs the immune system. It is fear that causes a person to back away and lose his or her integrity under threat. When this happens the body also gives way to threatening influences, i.e. viruses.

Adrenal Glands

These store grief, the suppression of which leads to a victim complex. The adrenals produce the 'fight' or 'flight' responses which only confirm a person's belief that something in the world is 'out to get him'. When someone is unwilling to lovingly endure painful emotional experience, he or she reacts as if the world is responsible for these experiences and forgets that each person is completely responsible for the creation of his or her life.

Spleen

This organ holds apathy, failure patterns and death wishes. When a person experiences more difficulty than he or she can endure, firstly, he or she gives up and then, believes in failure, and finally loses the will to live. This condition leads to much sluggishness in the life, which is reflected by sluggishness in the circulation and digestive systems. One of the problems that arises when you are trying to release apathy from someone's consciousness, is that, because feelings have become dead, there is a tendency to intellectualise. It is important to remind the patient not to intellectualise, but to really feel the apathy and to lovingly endure it.

Gonads

The gonads store unconsciousness, or any experience in which a person has given up self-governance, for example the use of drugs or alcohol, undergoing anaesthesia or hypnosis or losing consciousness through injury. When self-governance is lost, it is easy for an outside energy to take control, so it is on this level that possession occurs. As Nature abhors a vacuum, all patches of unconsciousness (which exist as holes in the Aura) will have some form of possession attached to them (see Chapter 3).

In releasing the gonads, it is important not to react to the possessing entities, but to focus on the unconsciousness until the holes in the Aura are healed and the entities, therefore, must have been squeezed out.

The Major Organs and Meridians

Heart

The heart is associated with love; it is damaged by any distortions of love's expressions such as jealousy, possessiveness or selfishness. The original cause of damage is usually some heartbreak, or loss, which shatters a person's trust in love, and leads to fear of further loss.

Gallbladder

Damage to this organ is a precursor to adverse heart conditions. The gallbladder can also be damaged by fear of loss. It stores all the tensions resulting from lack of trust in life. A person can be in a constant state of tension if there is anxiety about the future. Such anxiety is usually the result of past experiences which have shattered trust. When dealing with a person who has gallbladder problems the time of conception is probably the most important period of his or her life to consider. If the parents were not in a positive state when the soul was conceived, then that soul has undergone the trauma of not being welcomed into incarnation and there would have been great disappointment and worry about how the parents were going to take care of the child.

Liver

The liver has many functions relating to the breaking down, storing and rebuilding of matter. One or more of these functions will cease to work if some area of a person's life breaks down and he or she cannot handle the task of rebuilding it. The liver stores feelings of being overwhelmed, together with anger, hate and resentment.

Lungs

These have two main functions: taking in life and expressing ideas through speech. Lung problems result when a person has been stifled in his or her expression or in some area of life. When a person is brought up in a situation where parents or older siblings behave in a stifling or overpowering way, the child, and later the adult, reacts in one of two ways. Either the person becomes loud and pushy, in order to be heard, which leads to overstimulated lungs, or else the person gives up and closes down communication, which leads to weak lungs.

Stomach

The stomach's function is assimilation; its metaphysical function is the assimilation of experiences and ideas. When a person feels that too much is happening and he or she is unable to take it all in properly, the stomach may break down. Often this condition is a result of some worry which creates a split between mind and emotions.

Pancreas

Since the pancreas deals with sugar, it is linked with the 'sweetness' of life. It is damaged by bitterness.

Kidneys

Water is symbolic of emotions, and as the kidney is the main water-processing organ, it deals with the processing of emotions. The kidneys store the fear that results from those emotional traumas which damage a person's vitality, enthusiasm and motivation. When fear is stored in this way, an individual will be unable to handle any further emotional experiences.

Bladder

Because the bladder releases water, its condition is a measure of a person's ability to outwardly express emotions. The bladder is weakened when a person finds difficulty in expressing feelings.

Small Intestine

This involves the final stage of digestion and beginning of absorption, and so provides the basis for building and growth. Similarly, it provides the basis for the building of personality, character, will and confidence, and reflects the most impressionable stages of life. Its function is disturbed when a person experiences embarrassment early in life.

Large Intestine

Since the intestines deal with solid matter their ability to function correctly gives a measure of how well a person is dealing with the more material 'core' issues in life. The large intestines also relate to letting go, or releasing things that have no more purpose. The inability to let go may stem from a fear of loss. Like the gallbladder, the large intestine is much influenced by the time of conception. It is also affected by the childhood experiences that shape a person's attitudes and personality.

Sexual Organs and the Circulation-Sex Meridian

The reproductive organs, this meridian and the muscles controlling the hips, reflect the ability to express sexuality. A child's attitude to relationships is conditioned by its early experience of the relationship between the parents. Where there was conflict between the parents this often leads to a person experiencing traumatic relationships later in life.

Sometimes problems in these organs can arise from the parents wishing for a child of the opposite sex.

Triple-Warmer Meridian

Weakness in this meridian is normally associated with some clash with authority, whether it is a parent, teacher, boss or some other authority figure. The weakness results directly from the person's experience of not being able to have his or her say (even though the person may be right) because the other person has a position of authority.

Parts of the Body

Back

The back reflects that which one wants to put behind one. Back pain can be the result of issues or past experiences that one wishes to forget or put to the back of the mind.

The lower back is that place of support from which one should find leverage and strength. Pain in that area can result when a person resents not having the support he or she thinks is needed to achieve something.

Spine

The spine represents the will. Distortions of the spine are a result of not maintaining one's vision, in the face of pressure from outside - thus allowing the will to be "bent". The terms 'spineless' or 'no backbone' are very significant. The dominance of a parent may cause the initial surrender and then the pattern may continue into marriage, at work, or with other personal relationships.

Neck

The neck is the most flexible part of the spine, and reflects the balance between will and flexibility. A stiff neck shows a rigid attitude. The saying 'so-and-so is a pain in the neck' correctly describes the tension felt in the neck when one's rigidly held concepts are challenged.

Hair

Hair growth is governed by the liver, and hair loss results from rigidly holding on to anger. Where a person needs to impose his will on others and prove his point, or continues to bring up past resentments we often (accurately) describe them as 'hard-headed'.

Hips

The hips act as a balancing point and reflect the creative energy associated with child-bearing and, also, our ability to stand on our own. The flexibility of the hipbone joint relates to feelings about personal freedom. These issues come together during adolescence, when the awakening of the sexual instinct gives us our first sense of separating from the direction of our parents expectations.

If we give in to our parents' control instead of finding our own direction, our hips do not develop properly. Hip deterioration can stem from sexual guilt but equally our hips may be affected if we feel guilt or resentment because we have allowed others to make decisions for us i.e. we have not expressed our power.

Breasts

The breasts represent sexuality and the nurturing aspect of femininity. In most societies, breasts are an obvious outward sexual symbol. They store a woman's feelings about her sexuality and how men see her. This part of the body is damaged by sexual trauma, repression or resentment due to role expectations.

Legs

The legs both support us and carry us forward. Problems arise when a person has lacked the courage to take a new step. Often this is because the person did not have the support he or she believed was needed.

Hands

Hands relate to giving and taking. Problems may develop where a person does not feel equal to others, and therefore cannot find the right balance between giving and taking, maintaining his own will or yielding. The imbalance may originate in an over-developed ego or in the loss of self-worth.

III

THE CHAKRAS

The chakras provide the link between our individuality and the greater forces from which we receive nourishment. There has been much disagreement about whether the chakras are situated at the front or at the back of the body. Also there are differing theories about the relationships that exist between the glands and the chakras. These dilemmas can be resolved if we understand that our subtle body is not just a reflection of our physical body, but has a greater purpose. We therefore limit our understanding of this purpose if we try to relate each chakra to a separate gland. For instance, the Crown and Third Eye Chakras both affect both the pineal and pituitary glands.

Each chakra is like an energy vortex which penetrates the body from front to back (or from top to bottom in the case of the Crown Chakra), with openings on both sides (see Figure 2-1).

This chapter also describes a spot on the skull called the Psychic Gate which connects us to energies in the environment. A description of the subtle energy field that surrounds the body, known as the Aura, is given at the end of the chapter.

Crown Chakra

This chakra has opposite openings at the top of the head and, to form our connection with the earth, in the soles of the feet. The energy channel thus formed between the Crown and the feet openings of the chakra can be considered the most important of the energy channels. All other chakra energy channels cross it.

The Crown-Feet channel is like the trunk of a tree, which has its roots in the Earth, and its head reaching towards the Sun. The other chakra channels are like branches which spread out from it, each branch having its own important function.

19

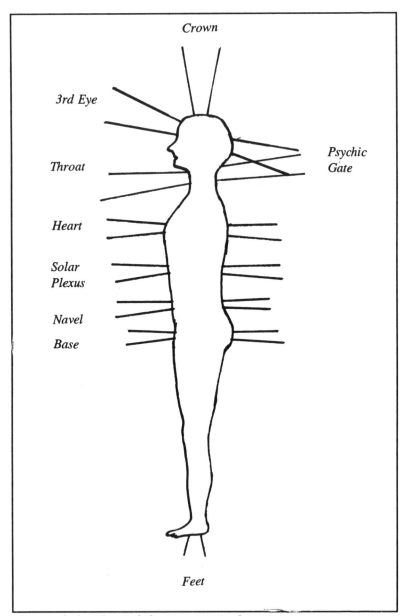

Figure 2-1: The Subtle Energy Body

The energy of this central channel is the energy of enthusiasm. The Crown is open to inspiration from beyond ourselves and the feet (our root) enable this force to be earthed. Those who believe we should close off from the material world in pursuit of enlightenment do not realise that the material world we experience is the manifestation of our inner consciousness. To escape from the material world is to escape from self and from our creator. Our spiritual evolution cannot be measured by the metaphysical concepts we are able to transmit to each other, but by our ability to create Heaven on Earth. This is only possible when the Crown Chakra channel is fully open.

We can see the connection between the spiritual and the material instincts when we look at how they are reflected in the body. For example the top-most cranial sutures hold the same patterns as the gonads. This is clearly seen in the physiology of the stag, whose horns are controlled by its sexual hormones.

We cannot open the Crown Chakra channel by denying the physical instincts, but only by uplifting and spiritualising them. We close the Crown opening of this channel whenever we deny the possibility of being inspired into action by powers greater than ourselves, and we close the feet chakras by losing our connection with the Earth. This can happen through over-idealism, loss of self-worth or by losing our will to other people.

Flower essences that help this channel are: Pennyroyal and Thistle for the Crown, Alfalfa for the feet, and Thornapple for the whole channel.

Third Eye Chakra

This chakra is considered to be the seat of the soul; it gives us our originality, our creative perception and our vision. We close it whenever we give up our own original, creative ideas to follow someone else's set beliefs. We can only have vision if we truly honour what we have been given. Since our unconscious self does not know the difference between self and others, this also means respecting other peoples' creative ideas. When a person loses his own ideas, jealousy causes him to undermine any other person's creative efforts. When the Third Eye is clear, we honour all creative, original ideas, in ourselves and others alike. When our inner vision opens, we find that what we first see in others is what is reflected in ourselves. We must remember that the purpose of Third Eye vision is not to look at others in judgement but to perceive life's meaning more deeply. For this to happen, we must shed many illusions. When we begin to honour our own vision, we start to release all the conditioning that we have accepted from the external world, layer by layer. It is said that the only clear view is from atop the mountain of our dead selves.

The flower essence which heals the Third Eye is Black Tulip.

Throat Chakra

This chakra allows expression and communication. Our abilities in these areas depend upon our sense of equality with others. If we feel that we are inferior we close down our power of expression. If we feel above others our communication is based on arrogance, loses truth and, therefore, loses power.

We damage our Throat Chakra whenever we place ourselves above or below another person, or when we fail to speak a truth when it was needed. When we see the divinity within all beings, we see that we are all equal. Comparison and judgement are distortions of the energy of the Throat Chakra based on lack of self-knowledge. This leads to fear of loss of self-importance.

Flower essences which heal the Throat Chakra are Forget-me-not, Alfalfa and Harebell.

Heart Chakra

The Heart Chakra governs our ability to give, after first receiving from the source. Just as our ability to give to others depends upon our love and compassion, our ability to receive nourishment from the source depends upon our self-love. The Heart Chakra energy gives us the ability to give unconditionally, as well as to attract what we need. Again, it is important to remember that the unconscious mind or lower self does not know the difference between self and others, so if we are to receive, we must wish the best for all others. Working with this energy we learn that power on all levels grows through giving, rather than receiving from others. If we become dependant on another we become weak towards that person. By giving to another we open ourselves to be replenished from the source.

An underdeveloped Heart Chakra leads to desire for power, selfishness and arrogance. When we lack self-love it is easy to form fixations on others as the source of our happiness. This is the cause of many heart breaks. True love gives unconditionally. If we give all we can to a person just because they represent possible fulfilment for ourselves, our giving is unbalanced and we do not replenish ourselves. In all problems of the Heart Chakra, self-love is the real issue.

Flower essences which heal the Heart Chakra are Apple and Wild Pansy.

The Lower Chakras

Each of the three lower chakras is a balancing point between complementary energies. The Solar Plexus balances the mind with the feelings, the Naval Chakra balances male and female energies, and the Base Chakra balances the energies of life and death.

Solar Plexus Chakra

This chakra gives us our sense of connectedness with others, and also provides personal power in dealing with others. It is a connecting point between the upper and lower body, between the mind and the instincts. If our conditioning is such that the beliefs held in the mind do not fit with our instincts and feelings, there is inner conflict and loss of confidence. The condition of our Solar Plexus Chakra, therefore, depends very much on our early conditioning and schooling. It can be blocked by anything that undermines our confidence, or causes disconnectedness to others or disconnectedness to our feelings.

Flower essences that heal the Solar Plexus Chakra are Dandelion, Sunflower and Cowslip.

Navel Chakra

The Navel Chakra is the centre of creative energy. This creativity is sometimes expressed as sexual energy, but the Navel Chakra makes no distinction between sexual energy and any other form of creative energy. In all things power flows between two opposite poles, and so the amount of creative energy available to us depends upon the interaction of male and female energies. The Navel Chakra is disturbed by any negative sexual conditioning, or any imbalance in human relationships, such as the dominance of one partner. This conditioning is often acquired in early childhood through observation of conflict within the parents' relationship.

The flower essence for healing the Navel Chakra is Scarlet Pimpernel.

Base Chakra

The Base Chakra is the foundation upon which all our other energies are built. It forms our connection with the physical world and is the source of our self-image and our survival instincts. The health and further development of the Base Chakra depends on an awareness of what we really are, and on our ability to accept death. It is the doorway through which life is brought into the world, and it is the connecting doorway between the realms of life and death. The relationship between life, sex and death is clearly illustrated by the increase in the sex instinct which is often observed when life is threatened. Dying men often ejaculate, and the most powerful aphrodisiacs are also deadly poisons. When we accept death we are able to live more fully, and when we overcome the fear of death we gain more confidence and self-worth. Any experience that decreases our self-worth damages the Base Chakra. We can overcome this by recognising our true eternal nature.

Flower essences that heal and develop the Base Chakra are Mandrake and Alfalfa.

A Note on Sexual Energy

Some authorities associate sexual energy with the Navel Chakra, and others associate it with the Base Chakra. However, it does not belong to either one of the chakras, but needs both of them in order to manifest. Sex is partly an expression of creative energy (which is characteristic of the Navel Chakra), partly a celebration of physical form (associated with the Base Chakra), and partly a doorway to bring in new life (which uses the energy of the Base Chakra). Sexual energy can be blocked by disturbances in either the Navel Chakra or the Base Chakras.

The flower essence for balancing the flow of sexual energy is Balsam Poplar.

The Psychic Gate

The Psychic Gate is a sensitive spot at the base of the skull through which we connect to energies coming from our environment. It is formed where the Third Eye Chakra and the Throat Chakra openings overlap at the back of the head.

Normally, we should be able to sense the energies of the environment without losing our self-governance, and, without losing discrimination. If our originality is not firmly based we tend to express the ideas of others, with the result that our Throat Chakra becomes a channel for the impressions that enter through the Psychic Gate. This opens us to manipulation by others and makes us vulnerable to the energies in our environment. The Psychic Gate will remain clear provided that the Third Eye Chakra and the Throat Chakra remain clear.

The flower essence for clearing the Psychic Gate is Butterfly Orchid.

The Aura

The Aura is an energy field that completely surrounds the body. It protects our energy system from interference from outside energies. Its strength depends upon the flow of energy through the Crown-Feet channel, much like the magnetic field that surrounds an electric wire. Weaknesses in the Aura often reflect lesions in the spine. Holes are made in the Aura wherever there is a gap in consciousness, i.e. when consciousness is surrendered to drugs, alcohol, anaesthetic, hypnosis or trauma. When this happens, the person has difficulty in disassociating himself or herself from other people and outside influences. In this case the person loses his or her own will, and may suffer many kinds of disturbance. Partial possession often occurs as outside energies fill the holes in the Aura. A person may be possessed by thought-forms or by spirits of other beings.

The flower essence for strengthening the Aura is Yarrow. The effect of this may be enhanced by taking it in combination with Thornapple, which acts on the Crown-Feet channel.

IV

TOOLS AND HELPERS OF A SHAMAN

With the right training you can receive help from the trees, and from spirit guides. For healing the Shaman uses healing wands, drums, rattles, herbs and flower essences.

Communicating with Tree Spirits

In order to develop a clear communication with tree spirits, there are three things we can do to prepare ourselves. First, develop an appreciation of trees, recognising all of their wonderful qualities; second, think about the benefits of developing this communication, in order to fire your enthusiasm for learning; and third, learn how to have the same attitudes as trees, to meet them on their own level. Once this preparation is done, there are some valuable techniques you can use for developing your communication skills.

Begin to appreciate trees by meditating on the following points: Trees have been our source of food, shelter and fire since the beginning of our evolution. They have sacrificed themselves for our growth and survival in many ways. Not only by inspiring man's use of fire, building materials, etc., but also by turning man's consciousness to something beyond his own selfish, blind plans. Observe how the trees that were destroyed by the hurricane of 1988 have awakened a new interest in ecology and a new care of Nature. It is no accident that this happened at the same time as the collapse of the stock market. This whole sequence of events was planned to shake mankind out of his blindness, and the trees had agreed to sacrifice themselves to aid our evolution.

Trees help our consciousness evolve in many ways. By inspiring poetry, creating love and peace, and by sheltering all who come under their branches. It is not surprising that lovers have always carved their initials into trees, since trees give out an aura of love. Compare the friendliness of country people to the

violence of our cities. Our souls cannot survive without trees any more than our bodies. And trees continue to give unconditionally, in spite of all our abuse of them. They are fully in tune with the Earth Mother at all times, being deeply rooted into the Earth. They give all of their fruit and leaves, not needing to withhold anything, trusting that more will grow again in Spring. Are they not a great example to us? Imagine the spiritual benefits of being in tune with these wonderful beings.

Apart from personal benefit, trees are a wonderful help in healing. Your healing skills will be enormously benefitted by using healing wands that have tree spirits living in them. All humans are fallible whereas the spirits of trees heal through their perfect, unconditional love, and natural attunement to the Goddess. We all act with less than unconditional love, and all lose our centres at times, so how can the energy we give to a patient be entirely healthy? Using a tree spirit as a healing tool overcomes this problem, ensuring that the patient receives the best, while guarding your own aura from unnecessary wear and tear and discarded psychic energies. The tree spirit also has a far deeper understanding of the soul than ours, and whatever amazing theories and practices healers dream up, there is always something beyond their limited understanding that is only known to Nature. Often healing occurs in unexpected ways when a soul is touched by Nature, and there are many examples of people who have begun new systems of healing and growth based on their experiences of this. Why follow another person's personal experience when you can go directly to the source itself?

Once you begin to appreciate these things, then you are ready to move on. The next step involves adopting a similar attitude to that held by trees. You do this by forming a good root and opening your heart. You can start forming your root by relaxing and letting your mind sink downwards. There are oriental teachings which teach you to form a root by concentrating your attention below the navel. Forget such things, mental exertion is not Nature's way. The mind comes to rest naturally in the lower abdomen when you are truly relaxed and aware of the Earth. Tension makes all your body rise up, so relax and let it sink. Relax the shoulders, let all your internal organs relax into the hips, and let your weight sink firmly onto the soles of your feet. Peoples' awareness tends to be centred too high. If you remember that the greater part of a tree is below the ground, your consciousness should reach about ten feet below you. If you allow yourself to sink and relax, your mind will rest naturally below the navel, and you will be able to feel the Earth's energy flowing through you. Become more sensitive with your feet so you are able to allow this to happen. The life force will then flow right through you, giving you nourishment, calmness and a strong centre.

Once the root is firm, your heart can open. Your heart may close because you feel vulnerable, because you are not secure enough in your own energy to handle what is happening around you. This can lead to emotional reaction and to judgement, and therefore you will not be able to open to unconditional love. Once the root is firm, the spirit is nourished by the Earth and therefore more secure. Then there is no need to fear or to judge others, or to make unreasonable demands from a position of insecurity. Opening the heart means that you have an attitude of non-judgement, you accept all things, even where these differ from your own limited view of the world. You show understanding, sensitivity and a willingness to listen and be aware of things that do not necessarily agree with your own conditioned belief system. Opening your heart enables you to shed your conditioning, but it requires a good root.

Imagine that your heart is the bud of a flower and that it is being nourished through your root. As it is nourished, the bud can open safely and show its full beauty. Let your sensitivity and acceptance open with it, and adopt an attitude of non-judgement.

When you get to this stage, you can begin to approach trees more on their own level. Approach a tree quietly with respect, be rooted, with your heart open, and begin to feel its presence. Approach from the North, as trees are more sensitive on the side where the Sun does not shine. From about fifteen feet away (although this may vary with the size and power of the tree) reach out and feel the Aura of the tree. Its Aura will have four layers, each layer separated by a few feet, with a fifth layer of energy within the bark. Be totally relaxed and feel very carefully for the first subtle layer of energy, and when you feel it, stop and introduce yourself. Then move closer slowly, with respect, feeling each layer of energy in turn, until you reach the trunk. Feel the fifth layer within the bark, keeping your awareness focused on the spirit, not just the physical. Next, whilst keeping your hands in contact with the tree, begin to circle it slowly in a clockwise direction. This is the direction in which the Sun, Moon and stars move, and it will help the tree accept you as a being within the natural order. During this time, begin to make a heart contact with the tree, share love, share your deepest feelings and secrets, treat it like a close friend. You can trust a tree never to tell anybody else. Let out all your guilt, and get past your barriers. When you feel open enough, and you feel the contact developing, feel which side of the tree is most welcoming and stop there. Hold yourself close to the tree for a moment, ask for its permission to share its energy then turn around and sit or stand with your back against the tree. Just relax into the spirit of the tree and let it fill you. Meditate with it for some time, and when you feel complete, lean forward to gently break the contact, and thank the tree before leaving.

It is good to gradually build up a relationship with the same tree, and to return at night under a full moon, when the contact will be at its strongest. Naturally, the quality of the meditation will vary from day to day and different feelings will come up as you gradually raise your vibration. Whatever you feel, be positive about it. Many suppressions will come up to be cleared, until gradually you develop a clear rapport with the spirit of love expressed through the tree.

There are certain flower essences you can take to help you through each stage. Chiming Bells will help your appreciation of trees and your recognition of love as expressed by Nature. Alfalfa will help develop your root. Wild Rose will help you open your heart and shed your conditioning. To aid the actual communication with nature spirits, take Green Bells of Ireland and Four-Leafed Clover.

There are a few popular misconceptions concerning tree magic. People are often advised to receive a gift from the tree, on a purely physical level, such as twigs or bark. To do this would put your focus on the wrong level. If you feel that you need a physical gift, then you are showing a lack of trust in the wonderful spiritual gifts the tree gives you. Do not acknowledge your lack of trust or sensitivity by demanding anything physical. Another practice that is common is to give the tree some kind of gift in return. What can you give to a being that receives all that it needs directly from the Goddess? If you need to give, question why you cannot receive freely and unconditionally. Or perhaps it is your humility that needs questioning. Do you imagine that you can give on the same level as Nature gives? We are all children to the Goddess, we receive all we have from her, and there is nothing we can give that is not already hers. So let the ego down, accept your total dependence, and let yourself receive graciously and humbly. If you wish to give anything, give your love and devotion.

Healing Wands

As your communication with tree spirits develops you will find that single branches call out to you and will wish to come with you. When this happens the dryad is sub-dividing, rather like an amoeba, so that a small dryad can inhabit a single branch. This tree spirit still has all the wisdom and experience of the parent dryad. Using your sensitivity, feel where you need to cut it, then saw off the branch and take it with you. To help the tree heal, patch up the cut with a little mud and spit. By attuning with the spirit in the branch, you should be able to tell how the wand needs to be trimmed and shaped. Finally, sand it smooth and polish with linseed oil and beeswax to help preserve it.

By meditating with the wand, you will gradually be taught how to work with it. There are limitless possibilities. You can use it for energy balancing on chakras, acupuncture points, etc., for psychic cleansing, or you may be shown a totally unique way of working. The tree spirit knows how it can best help you, so let it lead you for a while and learn from it. Eventually, you may collect a number of wands for many different purposes.

Do not go out looking for wands, however. Simply be open and sensitive and wait until a tree calls you to cut a wand. Gradually, a telepathic communication will develop and the trees may call you at any time. Avoid the need to cut wands to satisfy your intrigue or out of glamour. The Earth has suffered enough from mankind's greed for knowledge and power, especially since a new interest in shamanism has awakened. Mountains are being blown up to get more crystals, and endangered birds are being further threatened by those who want to get hold of their feathers. This cannot be considered as working in harmony with Nature. Do not let the same thing happen to tree spirits. If you wish to be more in tune with Nature, avoid buying such tools of power and accept what Nature gives you freely.

Spirit Guides

When you are healing others, as well as when you are working on your own growth, it is often useful to be able to communicate with a higher being to obtain guidance with those things that are currently beyond your ability. Each of us has a spirit guide whose purpose is to guide us through our life. This is normally another human soul who has been our teacher, guardian or guide in some previous life, and who has gone beyond this earthly plane. Before we come into incarnation, this guide will make a connection with us and gain an understanding of our purpose and whatever lessons we will face in our coming life. During our physical life, the guide is always watching over us, ready to remind us of our purpose and help us through our growth. We can also have many guides who come to help us because they are expert in a particular field of learning. These other guides may be evolved human souls, but can also be animal spirits or nature spirits. They will have their own special wisdom and power to pass on to you. Begin by making a connection with your personal spirit guide, and as your clairvoyance develops you will be able to speak with any other guides that come. You can even speak with other people's spirit guides and pass on guidance to them.

Remember that development of the Third Eye requires originality, so it is important to stop giving away power to other people. Leave behind any gurus or masters, and realise that no other human being is greater than yourself. If you spend your time trying to be enlightened by other people, you will never give the attention to your own inner source of teaching. Move away from the distraction of human teachers, and make the space to be alone with your guide. If you set aside some time each day to be with your guide, he or she will always be there, and even though you cannot see or hear anything, your vibration will gradually heighten through the guide's presence, until the time comes when you will be able to see and hear him or her.

Begin by drawing a circle around yourself and casting out the thought forms of other people. Then welcome your guide to you, and sit quietly, listening patiently. Be aware of any images that come into your mind. You may become aware of some other place such as a temple or grove, or some other special place in which you met your guide before. When this happens, remember the details of this place, and return to it in following meditations. This will be a step forward. It is in this place that you will first meet your guide. When your guide appears, note his or her looks, and try to find his or her name. Then sit with your guide for about twenty minutes each day until the connection is clear enough for you to be able to speak with him or her at any time.

It is important that you use this new gift wisely. Many

people get over-excited about channelled teachings, whilst ignoring many useful teachings that are not channelled. The truth is that many writings are inspired from other planes even though the writer may not be aware of this, whilst many channelled teachings are not pure, because they are filtered through the awareness of the channel. Most of the time, we are unaware of what external agents are working with us. There is always a mixture of our own consciousness with other consciousness. So having a channelled teaching is no guarantee that the teaching is pure. Being able to channel your spirit guide does not give you authority over other human beings. It is important to weigh up all teachings within your heart and see how they move you. But also examine your reasons for accepting or rejecting things. Most people reject teaching because it makes them feel uncomfortable rather than because the teaching is false. To discriminate clearly, it is important to accept the possibility that you may be wrong, and be willing to hear truths that are uncomfortable. Constantly strive to improve your connection with your higher consciousness, without insisting that you are right.

When guiding others, you will find that people ask all kinds of questions about their futures or about life's deeper meanings, many of which have no answer. People want to know the future because they are not happy with the present, but knowing the future does not change the present, whereas acting in the present can change the future. If you are asked questions about the meaning of life, again it is because the person is not fulfilled, and so wants to find an answer intellectually. The intellect alone will never bring fulfilment. It is the spleen/apathy pattern that causes someone to intellectualise, and it is good to realise this so that you can work on healing the real problem. This type of intellectualisation is just a form of escape, not much different from drugs or alcohol. The New Age junkie reaches for the tarot or crystal ball whenever he or she is down. Of course, there are always those who purport to give people the answers they seek, and succeed in disempowering them. By giving a person the authority to answer your deep questions, you give up power to them and so close your Third Eye. It is ironic that those who claim to function with an open Third Eye are often instrumental in closing the Third Eyes of others. If you are dedicated to real healing and the raising of consciousness, you will not lower yourself to such things. A Shaman is not a stage medium. Allow your guides to guide you to help a person in the best possible way.

The Higher Self

Just as we each have a guide, we also have a higher self. We have three minds, a conscious mind, a subconscious mind and a higher mind. The higher mind does not use words or feelings, but has a different kind of reasoning that is superior to both. Whereas a spirit guide has a personality and communicates with us on a human level, the higher self is less personal and does not use words, but imparts higher truths to us in another way if we are able to receive them. It can also impart the higher vital energy from its own level of existence. This energy is what really brings about spiritual transformation. So whilst the higher self can be our greatest helper, communication with it is the most difficult to master.

You can seek the contact using the same method as you used for meeting the spirit guide, by making the space for your higher self and allowing the contact to develop gradually. But now you must be open to non-verbal communication. The contact can be helped by accumulating vital energy through deep breathing. Offer up your breath to your higher self, see it rise to a few feet above your head where the higher self is traditionally believed to have its abode. In actual fact, the higher self has no limit in time or space, but because contact is made through the Crown Chakra, for all practical purposes it behaves as if it is located above the head. Offer up vital energy regularly.

Since the higher self works with unconditional love, compassion and for the greater good of all beings, the only other way of helping this contact to develop is by exercising compassion in your life.

Rattles and Drums

Often, in shamanic work, it is necessary to journey into other planes of consciousness. The transferral of consciousness is aided by sacred sound. In our lives we have two doorways between this life and the other plane; birth and death. The sound of the rattle, being produced by seeds within a womb-like structure, represents birth. The sound of the drum, being produced by the hide of a dead animal, represents death. These sounds can be used to help us journey between the planes.

The rattle is made from a female gourd and a stick taken from a male tree. Fill the gourd with seeds, and ram the stick into the hole. This is an obvious symbol of fertilization and birth. In use, the rattle is shaken in a circular fashion to produce a continuous sound.

The drum is made by stretching rawhide over a hollowed log. The height and width of the drum should match the height and width of the human head. The skin is stretched over both ends. The drum will then resonate with the head and be effective in altering consciousness. The skin is kept tight by heating, either in sunlight or in front of an open fire. In use the drum is beaten at a constant rhythm of approximately twice per second. You then 'ride' on the sound to reach other planes. The drum is the most common instrument for journeying.

Rattles can be used to bring a person back into normal reality, or to bring in other energies that may be useful, such as power animals or allies. Different rattles can be kept for different purposes.

Herbs

In the same way that a herb can be taken physically to heal physical disturbances, its spirit can also be taken to bring about healing on a deeper level. Since all physical conditions have their root in consciousness, in order to effect healing permanently the consciousness must change. In shamanism we always work with the spirit of the plant either by storing the spirit alone in a flower essence, or the whole herb can be taken with its spirit. This latter technique is similar to taking live wood wands. Of course, it requires the co-operation of the plant spirit. If you have developed a good communication with tree spirits, you can begin to work with smaller plants. Be sensitive and see which plants call you, then enter into quiet communication with the plant and see what it has to bring you.

A plant can tell you itself much about its deeper healing uses but there are other guidelines to help you understand how to use healing herbs. Since the physical condition is a perfect reflection of consciousness, then, similarly, the physical administration of the herb will heal the physical illness and its spirit will heal the emotional or mental condition that is at the root. Plants have had to adapt to many environmental difficulties and can give us the qualities we need to deal with similar difficulties. As an example, the first plant I used in this way was the Dandelion, to help my liver. I noticed that the Dandelion had a large root, so it was 'earthy'; its bright yellow flower represented the Sun, and its white sap represented the Moon. It had no scent. The only element it lacked was air. I realised that this was like my birth chart, because I have no planets in air. This meant that I found it difficult to express myself, which in turn created frustrations that built up in the liver. The Dandelion spirit strengthened my root and my vital energy and provided a calm understanding of my emotions, which overcame the problem. It did not provide the missing air element- that came later from another plant - but it gave me the ability to cope with what I was.

To work with plants in this way, you must be open to the particular plant the spirit is offering you, so that you can take it live, with the spirit still in it.

It is beyond the scope of this book to describe the use of all the different herbs. However, if you study any herb and look symbolically at the conditions that it can be used to treat, this will lead you to the inner cause of the condition. Go out and observe the nature of the plant, you will quite easily discover its healing virtues.

Here are a few more herbs for healing the organs described in Chapter 2.

Mullein

This herb is used for the spleen. Its thick, soft leaves are very earthy, and its light yellow flowers represent the intellect. The negative qualities of earth are inertia, sluggishness and apathy, all conditions which damage the spleen. These build up as a person is undermined or defeated, or when life becomes too hard. When a person gets into a state of apathy, he or she escapes from feeling by intellectualising. Mullein brings the positive earth qualities - stability and endurance - which can overcome the inertia. The positive side of the intellect is its ability to hold inspired ideas, which will help motivate an apathetic person. Mullein is by far the best herb for this purpose.

Hawthorn

Either the flowers or the berries of the Hawthorn can be used for the heart. Traditionally Hawthorn protects the innocent until they are fully awake. It is the innocent heart, not yet experienced in the harshness of the world, which falls most deeply in love, and is also most hurt when love fails. These deep hurts lead to heart disease, and can also lead to cancer. The spirit of Hawthorn soothes and heals the emotional wounds that damage the heart.

The scent of the Hawthorn brings feelings of innocence, and the thorns bring pain.

Nettle

The nettle is used for the blood, the spine and the marrow, because its fiery nature strengthens the will. Often, when clearing spinal lesions, some vertebrae need to be decalcified (a process thought impossible by most medical authorities, but which occurs naturally when the underlying emotional stress is identified), and decalcification requires a lot of minerals. Nettle provides a concentration of natural minerals in perfect balance. Lesions in the spine reflect those times when the will of the person has been bent, and nettle is a very fiery, strong-willed plant. As it overcomes the ravages of outside influences upon the person's consciousness, this is reflected in the casting out of toxins from the blood. Nettle is known as an excellent blood-purifier.

Lobelia

This is used for the lung. Lung conditions arise as a result of a person being stifled, and the person can react either by closing down communication or by becoming excessively loud and pushy. Lobelia is excellent for balancing this state as it contains both stimulant and relaxing qualities. The flowers are blue (representing the Throat Chakra and, therefore, outward expression), and two-tipped (representing the mouth, again outward expression). Lobelia grows only in acid soil, reflecting the environment and the type of people that originally affected the person's expression.

Comfrey

This herb is used for the bowels. Bowel troubles originate in very old emotional disillusionment. A person lost trust in love and life, and holds on to resentment, which he or she is unable to release.

This person is stuck in old times, not moving forward with new life currents. The healing virtue of Comfrey stems from its relationship with time. Comfrey is traditionally associated with Saturn, but its pale purple or cream coloured flowers, and its tendency to grow in wet shady places also suggest a strong lunar influence. It brings us into harmony with the rhythms of life, and helps us to be present and move forward to what is new. It, therefore, helps break us out of living in the past and enables us to let go. This is a very important part of the process which frees us from emotional blocks, just as the intestine is a very central organ which can affect all the surrounding organs. Apart from being an excellent intestinal cleanser and healer, Comfrey has much virtue in healing all kinds of wounds and injuries.

Dandelion

Apart from healing the liver, Dandelion is also used for the kidneys. The kidneys' main function in filtering urine is to discriminate between waste products and nutrients. Kidney weakness usually stems from insecurity. An insecure person normally loses discrimination in his or her anxiety to meet his or her needs and in guarding against anything that threatens. In desperately seeking help, the person leaves him or herself open to harmful or abusive influences. In protecting him or herself the person may shut out much that would be beneficial. Dandelion can centre such a person and bring about a calm understanding of emotions, thus restoring him or her to a position of discrimination in which security may be gradually rebuilt. It is interesting to note that many diuretics deplete the body of valuable minerals. Dandelion, on the other hand, supplies these minerals in abundance, and is therefore the most perfect diuretic.

Walnut

This is used for the sexual glands. The green shells boiled in water are an old remedy for impotence. The gonads are weakened by unconscious states and unconscious external forces, which enter a person's Aura whenever self-governance is lost. The walnut looks like a brain, with a hard shell protecting it. The brain is the centre of our consciousness and the gonads reflex the upper part of the brain. Walnut's effectiveness stems from its ability to protect consciousness from external agencies. Note the use of the Bach Flower remedy as a protection remedy.

Flower Essences

Although flower essences do not have the physical qualities of the whole herb, they have several advantages. First of all they have a longer shelf-life. Many flower essences can be made up and stored indefinitely, ready to be used when needed. Secondly, there are many poisonous plants that can help us in our growth and healing, and these obviously cannot be taken physically. With poisonous plants, it is not a case of interpreting their physical healing properties, we must observe what challenges the plant has faced in its development and how it has adapted to cope with them. Poisonous plants have a special power in that they have developed a poison which gives them a certain immunity to the kind of abuse that might be suffered by other plants. They can, therefore, lend great strength to our spirits when we are under threat. Each species will act in a different way. Belladonna can guard against any psychic influence. It acts as a kind of psychic purge, quickly freeing one of any psychic influences. Stinking Hellebore works more on the emotional level. It gives one the strength to deal with emotional 'attacks', whilst keeping one's heart open. Mandrake helps us find our own source of strength by showing us that which is eternal and indestructible within us.

Henbane and Thornapple are more initiatory, and are used for entirely spiritual purposes.

Flower essences are extremely versatile, and can help in many areas, apart from that considered as healing. But we need to be more intuitive in working with them because fewer clues are provided by their physical properties. We need to develop our communication with plant spirits to such a degree that we can learn all we need to know entirely by 'talking' to them. This will come through practice.

Preparing Flower Essences

To prepare flower essences, first of all see which plant is calling you and which of its flowers it is offering for your use. Take only those flowers that it is giving freely. If your intuition is less than perfect, you can get confirmation by noticing how easily the flowers come away in your hand. When the plant is offering its flowers, they come away easily. When the plant has given enough, it suddenly alters its chemistry so that the flowers are harder to pick. So if the flower is suddenly harder to pick, leave it. If you force things, you will not have the full co-operation of the plant spirit.

Next, place the flowers face down on the surface of a shallow dish of water (the water should be no more than half an inch deep), covering the surface. This allows a high concentration of energy in the water. Stand the dish in sunlight next to the plant, and ask the plant spirit to bless the water with its qualities. Leave it standing in direct sunlight for about three hours, or longer if it is not a sunny day. When you feel that the spirit has entered the water, thank the plant and then scoop off the flowers from the surface of the water. Use a leaf to do this, so you do not contaminate the water with any other energy. Mix the water with equal parts of brandy to preserve it, and store it somewhere quiet for a few days while the spirit adapts to its new environment. Remember that this essence is alive, and should be treated with the same respect as the plant. This is the 'Mother Essence'. After a few days you can make a stock by adding seven drops of the Mother Essence to a 10ml bottle containing a mixture of spring water and brandy. For the stock to last a long time, it needs to be at least half brandy. Though there should always be some spring water to keep the essence alive. The new stock is almost like a newly born child, and needs to be left with the 'Mother' for a few days. This allows the spirit to separate slowly without shock, and leads to a happier, more effective remedy. After a few days, the stock is ready for use. A remedy bottle can be made up by adding two drops of the stock to about one ounce of spring water. The patient should normally take four drops, four times a day. Otherwise, the stock can be placed on the body and worked into the Aura. This is described in Chapter 6: "Infusing a Positive Pattern".

There are manufacturers of flower essences who would not bother with all these rules for the production of their essences, because they need a faster process to allow mass production. Such essences never produce spectacular results. They are a very pale reflection of essences prepared in the proper way. A good essence can bring about great transformation. It makes all the difference to gain the co-operation of the plant spirit.

V

BUILDING SHAMANIC POWER

Power is born of peace, but requires resistance in order to develop. This implies that our training must encompass apparent opposites: deep relaxation and a certain amount of hardship. We see this reflected on the physical plane, where we need rest and sleep to maintain our health, and we also need exercise to develop strength. The more resistance our muscles have to work against, the more they grow. A body builder is willing to put up with a certain amount of discomfort in order to grow strong. The same is true of the Yogi, but in a different way. When you are not used to stretching, it is rather uncomfortable and difficult, but as you persevere you become fitter and healthier. Plants, too, grow stronger if they grow against resistance. Plants growing in the wind tend to be much stronger. The same is true on the emotional and mental planes. The mind is developed through study and concentration, but it needs relaxation and meditation to nourish it. Emotional pain tends to lead to a more compassionate nature, provided we find enough love to face the pain.

Life has been given to us as a wonderful gift; it provides us with the inner spark to take us forward, as well as plenty of opposition and resistance to help us grow. It is, therefore, bound to contain both pleasure and discomfort. In order to grow in balance, we need to accept the difficulties and pains of life, since they will come to us anyway.

It is the love, inner nourishment, and willingness to grow that enables us to lovingly endure all difficulties. Any good spiritual training programme needs to provide inner nourishment as well as a certain amount of hardship, because by willingly setting ourselves against hardship we are able to lovingly and willingly face the hardships of life.

Those people who try to avoid discomfort and who complain about the problems that come their way are on a constant downward path. This attitude leads to a victim complex and continuous emotional wallowing. Your first step towards shedding victim patterns and taking on your true power demonstrates also your willingness to face opposition and pain in order to grow. This will not only benefit you, but will also flow to those on whom you practice healing. You cannot command a patient to grow, you can only inspire them. The more you manifest your inner power, the more you inspire others to reach for their true strength.

The exercises in this section contain gentle meditations to nourish your soul, as well as a few harder ones to give you some difficulty to work against. The harder exercises are not intended to make you work so hard that you become stressed or want to give up; go on with the gentler exercises until you feel enough inner nourishment to handle the difficult ones with love, so that you are always working with a positive attitude.

Exercise 1 - Developing the Root

If you have carried out the exercise with the trees, described in the previous chapter, you already will have some experience of rooting yourself. We will now develop this a little further. Begin by relaxing and sinking in the normal way, but then visualise roots spreading out of your feet and deep into the ground as if you were a tree.

The first time, try to see your roots going about ten feet into the ground and feel how solid this makes you. Each time you do this exercise, turn your mind a little further down below the ground, until you can see your roots going on for miles. Visualise it as clearly as you can, as if you could actually see into the earth. Eventually, see your roots reaching down into the Underworld, which is where the darker side of yourself resides, together with all that you have suppressed. This will help you to integrate these things within your consciousness, which is an important step in finding your full power.

Many students of shamanism learn to journey into the Underworld in a trance state in order to find power. This is all very well, but in order to function efficiently in the real world, particularly if you are working with other people, you need to be able to draw upon these powers while in normal waking consciousness. Practising the rooting exercise will enable you to directly draw power from the Underworld up through your roots so this makes it more important than the journeying method.

The next stage involves performing the exercise kneeling rather than standing. Kneel with your big toes touching, your insteps flat on the floor, and your knees wide apart, so that your legs form an equilateral triangle. The distance between your knees should be the same as the length of your calf. Let the hands rest palm down on the thighs. The spine should be straight but relaxed. This is an extremely stable position (the equilateral triangle is a symbol of stability) and it will give you a greater understanding of your root. It is also a much better position for your spine than any sitting position.

At first it will be uncomfortable, and you may want to rise up rather than sink down into your root. However, try to relax into the discomfort, sink and find your root. The stiffness of the muscles is actually a measure of your resistance to being rooted. If you have ever studied Kinesiology you will realise that each muscle is reflected to some organ or energy system. Each of the muscles being stretched down the front of the legs has some reflex action to your root, and stretching these muscles will gradually overcome the resistance. So, as you relax into the position you work through any resistance to being rooted and grow stronger.

The next stage of the exercise is to see the roots as an extension of your whole body instead of just growing out of your feet. Visualise a thick root the width of your body, going deep into the earth, and try to deepen it a little each day. Practice this regularly so that you can gradually stay for longer and longer periods of time, and, eventually, you will be able to practice all your meditations in this position.

Exercise 2 - Breathing

Breath is the source of Life, and, if used consciously, it can empower us and still the mind. Begin by imagining yourself to be the centre of the universe. In actual fact, you are! In an infinite universe any point can be the centre. Consider that you have infinity above you, infinity below you, and infinity to every side so that you are the centre of an infinite universe. If you are relaxed and rooted, the centre of your being will be in the lower abdomen, just below the navel. You are going to draw the breath of the universe into this point.

Start by emptying the lungs then, as you slowly breathe in, feel that you are breathing the whole universe into this one point below the navel. Do not use the upper chest too much, feel the lower abdomen expanding first, so that you remain rooted. When you are full, begin to breathe out through the mouth, visualising the breath going out across the world and over the horizon, then beyond the world and out to the stars, and beyond again to infinity. When that breath is complete, let go of its energy, having sent it to infinity, and again draw all the breath of the universe into the lower abdomen and, then, once more, extend it to infinity. Continue for as long as you like.

Practice this breathing exercise in the kneeling position described above. Strive to make your breathing slower and deeper, whilst remaining firmly rooted. Deepen and slow down your breath to such an extent that the only way to prevent straining is by concentrating on sinking into your root; in this way you are using the strength of your root to conquer the difficulty. Aim to eventually take thirty seconds for each in breath and thirty seconds for each out breath. Try to maintain it for a little longer each day.

Exercise 3 - Finding Stillness

This exercise is a pre-requisite for the development exercises described later because it will enable you to still the mind and listen to a deeper aspect of your consciousness.

At first, you need to perform the exercise in a quiet place in Nature. Choose a hill where you can climb out of reach of any noise or distraction, and where you can have a clear view out into open space. Begin the exercise a few days after a New Moon, so that you can watch the moon setting. Climb the hill in the evening to watch the sunset. Notice how birdsong changes at this time, in preparation for sleep. The sounds are almost an invocation of stillness. Watch the sun setting, be aware of how the energy changes from day to night, as the solar power gives way to the lunar power. Watch the crescent moon for a while and be aware of its subtle, quiet, intuitive nature, until it too sets below the horizon, giving way to an even deeper stillness. Now allow your mind to settle in the total darkness and stillness of the Void. Repeat an invocation such as the following:

Lord of Death, Eternal One, grant me thy power
Thy strength, born of the Void, be in me this hour
Bring me thy stillness, show me my source
My silent centre, that greatest force
Bring into my being thy vastness and might
So subtle, hidden behind day and night
Deepen my understanding, feeling and sight
Let me encompass thy depth and height
Welcome me into thy realms so great
The realms behind life and death, that give me my fate
Teach me thy wisdom, nourish my soul
Fill me with power, aid me in my goal
To encompass death, that I may truly live
To be thy priest, thy blessings to give
To deepen my spirit to know my destiny

To be secure in my connection with thee
Show me that which is eternal in me
Grant me thy vision that I may see
Keep me still, secure and strong
Let me grow stronger, my whole life long
Show me thy eternal power to vanquish all fears
So I may come to unite with thee through all the eternal years

Then spend some time just listening to the silence. After this, contemplate the fact that all the miracles of Nature occur in silence. You cannot hear the buds appearing on the trees, or the grass growing, the Sun rising and setting, the stars appearing or the corn ripening.

When you have experienced a profound stillness and feel that the exercise is complete for this day, thank the spirit of stillness and then return home. (Remember to bring a torch so that you can find your way back in the dark!)

Then, perform the exercise after you have fasted for a few days. Fasting allows the body to reach a greater degree of stillness, and what occurs in the body is reflected in the mind. You may find, however, that as your energy changes during the fast you will have less control over the mind; it will be all over the place. Don't force anything, this is a time for rest and peace. The mind will settle down as you listen to the silence. It will be slower to reach stillness but will be able to reach a deeper level now, which will have a more permanent effect. Be sure to be warmly clothed because the body temperature can drop.

Finally, having succeeded in finding stillness, begin to practice in noisier places. Pick the noisiest place you can find where you will not be in any danger, perhaps close to the side of a busy motorway or next to an industrial site. Do not resist the noise, just relax, sink into your root and listen to it. Spend time listening to the more obvious noises, and then pay attention to any other sounds in the background. Then listen to the silence that lies behind all the sounds. After listening for a while, the same sense of stillness that you felt on the hill should come back to you. By

Building Shamanic Power

practising in this way, you will find a profound and powerful stillness which no noise can disturb.

Exercise 4 - Clairvoyance and Psychometry

This exercise will help you to diagnose and find the root cause of any problem, in yourself or in others. It works through the Heart Chakra, which enables you to feel all that is true. If you performed the exercises with tree spirits as described earlier, your Heart Chakra will have developed to some degree already.

It is best to begin practising this exercise sitting under a tree with which you have a good connection. Start with your eyes closed, and take a moment to relax, find your root and become still. Begin to be aware of your heart. Visualise your heart as the bud of a flower. As this flower is nourished by your root, it gradually begins to open. Allow it to open completely, feeling a great sense of beauty flowing from it. Now imagine you are looking out from the centre of this flower, and from here you can see all things on all levels. Look up and down yourself with the intention of finding any disharmonies. When you are drawn to a particular area, focus your attention on it to feel what the disharmony is. It may be some suppressed emotion, or it may be a disturbance to your vital energy in the form of some psychic contamination or a negative psychic link (an 'aka cord') to another person. Whatever it is, look deeper and find out how old it is, i.e. how long your energy has been disturbed in this way. Then let your heart tell you how it came about. You may then remember some emotionally difficult event. Let yourself feel the emotion, and intensify it rather than push it away. Open your heart to fully accept the event, without resistance or judgement. If you can see an 'aka cord', visualise a knife and cut it. If energy has been taken from you, command it to come back. If there is any negative influence on you, will it to return to its source. It is quite possible that you will have memories from a past life, as well as

51

memories from your present life, and they can be dealt with in the same way. Practising this exercise will free you of your own mental and emotional blocks, as well as developing your intuition. This technique can also be used on others. If you have someone to practice with, have them sit quietly while you close your eyes and touch the palm of his or her hand. This is an easy way to begin sensing another person's energy. If you do not have an understanding subject to practice with, sit alone and mentally attune with someone you know. Take a moment to centre yourself and open your heart, and then reach into the other person with your feelings. It is as if you are looking out from the flower of your heart into the other person. Don't be passive and just wait for impressions to come, reach out and search the person for emotional blocks or other disturbances. Feel what kind of feelings the person is holding on to, and what traumas have affected him or her. If you have a willing subject, tell him or her what you find so that it can be confirmed.

You can extend this exercise using the "unmasking" technique. You must first realise that we all wear a mask which hides our true nature. We see this truth demonstrated when people suddenly show a new side to themselves which shocks everyone. When crimes are committed, the criminal's family and friends find it hard to believe the person capable of such things. Similarly, many people fall prey to confidence tricksters. And there are many people putting on brave faces and hiding much inner suffering, unknown to their acquaintances. The problem is that we have learned to only take notice of a person's face and words as a guide to his/her inner thoughts and feelings, instead of reaching out with our hearts. Since our perception of a person's face can lead to much illusion, we need to eradicate its effect on our inner vision. We do this by visualisation. Realise that whoever you are looking at is wearing a mask. In your mind, reach out and pull the mask off. Avoid any tendency to see another face beneath the mask, since that would be just another layer of illusion. The only information we can rely on is that which we feel deep within our hearts. Once you have removed the mask, do not focus on the face at all, but reach into the person with your feelings and sense what is inside them. Learning to do this will enable you to be more complete in your healing. You will not miss any important problems that need dealing with, and you will also be safe from other peoples' hidden intentions.

Exercise 5 - Inner Journeying

This is perhaps the most commonly known of all shamanic practices. The Journeying technique deals with travel to the Astral plane, where all physical events have a cause. The value of journeying to you as a healer is that it will enable you to deal with the elemental energy of mental or emotional blocks, limited beliefs and restricting habits.

All events and all thoughts carry a certain amount of elemental energy. Most of these energies are weak and soon disperse. However, a traumatic event which has a great deal of emotional content will form a stronger energy pattern which remains in a person's Astral environment. If the emotions are repeated in other circumstances, this pattern will be reinforced. Such an energy pattern will tend to perpetuate itself by leading the person into further emotionally charged events. In this way a habit which is very difficult to break can form, or a pattern of events can re-occur in one's life. Methods of counselling, regression therapy and stress release do not heal the pattern, because we are not just dealing with emotions, memories and thought patterns, there is also a powerful elemental energy compelling the person to behave in a certain way, and inflaming the emotions. By entering the Astral plane and removing or changing the elemental energy of the pattern, the pattern can be healed quickly and completely.

In shamanism, it is normal to view the inner planes as if they were located on two levels, an Underworld and an Upperworld. Although the inner planes are not really limited to a physical direction, for all practical purposes, the planes behave as if they are below and above us. Think of it like this: our material world is surrounded by a Formative plane, and beyond that there is a still more subtle plane we can call the Creative plane. Beyond that there is an unlimited source, we can call the Void, the Source or the Divine Essence. The first plane we enter is that which exists just beyond birth or death. Our doorway to this plane is through the Base Chakra, which is our point of passage between life and death. Our shamanic technique for entering this plane consists of projecting down through our root. For this reason we know it as the Underworld. To enter the next plane, we must go beyond emotions, personality etc. which means, in a way, going through a kind of second death. To do this we must be able to trust totally in something which is beyond our limited selves. This requires a developed Crown Chakra. Since our doorway to this plane, therefore, is through the Crown Chakra, our shamanic technique consists of projecting upwards and, therefore, we call this plane the Upperworld.

However, in order to reach the Upperworld we have to first travel through the Underworld. The Underworld is normally associated with the depths of the Earth, our Great Mother. The Upperworld is associated with the stars above us, the sources of light, and our even older Mother of which the Earth is a child, since the Earth is created out of a star. The Void can be associated with the darkness beyond all the stars and galaxies. We can feel what it is like to journey through these different planes by imagining ourselves sinking deep into the Earth. As we sink deeper, we get more and more in touch with older parts of ourselves, so that the further down we travel, the further back in time we regress. When we get far enough back we will reach the time of the formation of the Earth. When we reach the time when the Earth was just part of a star, we will find ourselves out amongst the stars. We have now shifted from Underworld to Upperworld. As we continue to journey back in time we go beyond the stars, before the creation of the universe, to find the source from which we came. Here we can go beyond all our limits and find an infinite source of power.

We need to do our healing in the Underworld. This is our subconscious, and the collective unconscious. Here we find all our fears, limitations and suppressions. Here are all the demons of hell - which are nothing more than the elemental energies we have drawn to ourselves. We can control and cleanse our Underworld by shedding our limitations and gaining the higher powers that are available to us in the Upperworld. However, because we always have to travel through the Underworld to reach the Upperworld, when we journey for the first time, we are immediately faced with the problem of dealing with the difficult energies of the Underworld before we have had the opportunity to gain help from the higher powers of the Upperworld. This problem can be solved by connecting, via the collective unconscious, to those beings in our Underworld who can act as our guardians. The purpose of our first trip to the Underworld, therefore, should be to gain a guardian or ally. This help usually comes in the form of an animal spirit (your power animal) which knows how to look after you in the Underworld. If you have gained the friendship of a tree spirit through earlier work, this can also help you in your journeying.

Here is a method of inner journeying. The sound of the drum beat is a great aid to entering the Underworld; if you are alone you will need a tape recording of drumming since you have to lie down and completely relax to perform the journey. Have it playing throughout the journey. Begin with some ceremony or prayer of cleansing and protection (see the example at the end of this section). Once you are in a safe and clear space, switch on the drumming and lie down and relax. You should be in darkness or low lighting. Breathe deeply and slowly for a while, without strain. Feel your body relaxing completely. Gradually drift away from physical reality by visualising some relaxing place in Nature. When the visualisation is easy and vivid, find a hole in the ground that goes deep down, and is wide enough to get into. Climb into the hole and journey down it, going deeper and deeper into the Earth. Continue down this tunnel for as long as you need to, until the scenery changes and you find yourself in another plane. This is the Underworld. The first thing you should do is look for a guardian spirit to help you. Over time, you might gain many animal and plant spirits who will help you in different ways, and will be able to deal with any difficulties you face in the Underworld. In the Underworld you might find thought-forms that need to be broken down, entities to be released, or parts of yourself that are lost and need to be brought back. I cannot give you specific instructions about this because what you find is entirely personal, but by now you should have developed a fair amount of intuition and inner guidance.

However, you will almost certainly find some problems you cannot overcome until you have been to higher planes. When you have become proficient at Underworld journeying you can travel to higher planes by sinking further back in time (as described above) until you get to the time of the Earth's formation and find yourself amongst the stars. You will have gone beyond the thought-forms and limitations of the Underworld, into a dimension of light. Each star is a different source of Light, or a different doorway. You can travel to any one of them to absorb higher spiritual energies, and to meet higher beings. You may gain the help of a guardian angel.

The most distant level of journeying takes you beyond the stars; you continue to journey further and further back to the time before the Universe was created. When you reach the Source, there is no light and no form, for it is beyond all that. You may see some colour, which in some way represents your current relationship to the Source, or you may simply experience the Void. Whatever the case there will be an incredible sense of peace and power. Because the Source is formless, there is nothing you can do except be there, experience it and absorb it. When you have done so you will find it much easier to shed your conditioning and realise your limitless power.

Always complete your journey by returning the same way you came, i.e. back through the stars, to the centre of the Earth and back up the tunnel to your body lying on the ground. Follow this kind of inner work with some physical exercise as a balance.

A traditional method is to spontaneously dance your power animal. Afterwards it is also good to do some rooting exercises and breathing.

In order to become proficient at underworld journeying, or any kind of astral travel, it is important to develop the Base Chakra, and become strongly rooted. It is often thought that unearthed people function better on the Astral plane, but this is not necessarily true. Such people usually are neither fully present in the material world, nor do they have any control on the Astral. Their Astral experience is likely to be negative, as they are open to influence by Astral entities. On the other hand, those who develop a strong centre are able to function on the Astral with more control and clarity, partly because their vital energy and will are more highly developed, and partly because they are more able to relax deeply and fully let go. It is therefore important to practise the rooting exercises and to overcome one's fear of death. It is also important to avoid any drugs that affect consciousness, as these damage the root by taking away self-governance. Some people use drugs as a means of opening up to the other planes, but the drugs only take them to a limited plane, and therefore do not give a true sense of reality. Furthermore, drugs limit your ability to shift consciousness naturally, and open you to be influenced by your Astral environment.

Purification and Banishing Ritual

The following ritual will clear negative astral influences. It can be performed every night before sleep, or before inner journeying. The ritual requires no equipment. Just follow the words, which are written in verse because this ensures that both sides of the brain are used. Accompany it by drawing a circle around yourself using your hand, beginning in the East, circle clockwise, and then draw a banishing pentagram to each quarter. The pentagram is drawn by beginning in front of your left hip, tracing upwards to head height, down to the right hip, across to the left shoulder, then across to the right shoulder, and back to the start.

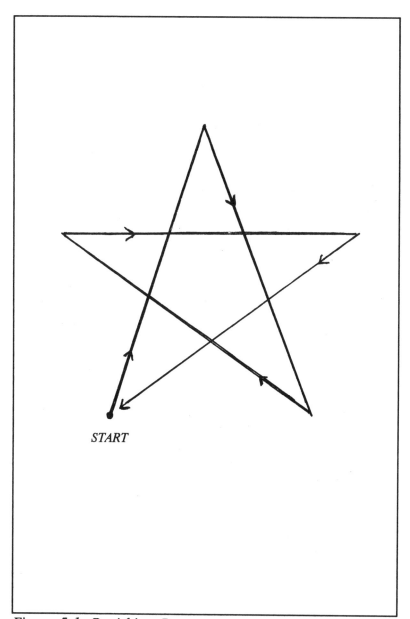

Figure 5-1: Banishing Pentagram

Shamanic Healing

This is the invocation:

Goddess, to thee I call, in thee I believe
I open my heart, thy power to receive
Grant me thy presence, let me feel thy grace
Help me to cleanse and bless this space

Consecrate this place to thy holy name
And lend me thy power to do the same
Let it be thy presence that keeps me still
As I charge all present to obey thy will

The presence of the Goddess is about to appear
So let this space be pure and clear
All dross and creatures of decay and strife
Go, lest ye profane the source of life

O Goddess, now let thy presence be fully known
Within my heart, where is found thy throne
Manifest here, show us thy will
Guide our work and keep our spirits still

In recognition of thee I draw this ring
So within it thy gifts thou may bring
Grant that it may keep us free
Of all that is not at one with thee

Great Goddess, as we receive thy gifts from above
Of light and life and strength and love
We pray that you may guard our souls
And keep us aligned to our rightful goals

As we stand firm upon the earth
We recognise the Goddess who gave us birth
And accept the life that flows from below
Enabling us to truly grow

(East)
Goddess, grant me now the power of air
And the protection of thy spirits fair
Grant that nothing shall pass this gate
That is not aligned to my true, noble fate

(South)
Goddess, grant me now the power of fire
To protect all that is your heart's desire
May the guardian of the south stand firm and clear
To protect all that we hold dear

(West)
Let thy watery power guard this western door
So that thy blessings can truly pour
Into our lives, into this space
That we may feel thine infinite grace

(North)
Let thy power guard the portal of North
So nought but love may pour forth
To fill our minds, our hearts, our souls
And hold us firm in our greater goals

My space is now dedicated to these principles four
Above me light, below me life, within me love, around me law
Maintained by the guardians of each elemental door
And that one great source that I stand for

Goddess, now you protect this space
And so we surrender to thine infinite grace
And thank thee for giving us the room
Within thy safe, encompassing womb

Exercise 6 - Past Life Regression

This is a technique which can be used on others to find and release past traumas. However, it is useful to do it by yourself first, since this will help you to understand the process. The first time you perform this exercise, do it under a tree with which you have made a good connection, and ask the tree spirit to help you and keep you focused. Tree spirits are extremely useful helpers to have in any kind of time travel work; they do not have our limitations in time, since they live in past, present and future all at once.

Sit comfortably or lie down and relax deeply. Gradually let your mind go, and drift away from physical reality. Just think of the darkness and emptiness of space, as if you were out in the Void. See below you a large spiral staircase, winding down and down into the darkness. This spiral represents time, and you can consider each step as one year. Begin to walk down the staircase, realising that you are walking back in time, gradually going down further and further into the past. Be aware of your intention to find a life which can help you to either understand and release some mental or emotional block, or to recognise your potential. Continue down the spiral of time until some previous life-time begins to unfold. Now just stop and observe. Be aware of how you are dressed, what environment you are in, and whether there is anybody else around. Just experience what happens for as long as you wish. If you experience anything traumatic try to lovingly endure it, without resistance, knowing that you can come out of it at any time. When you have finished, walk back up the staircase until you are back in the present once more, then slowly open your eyes and return to normal.

Exercise 7 - Discovering Your Own Death

Discovering your own death, and accepting it, is a good way to overcome fear. The experience will develop your Base Chakra and help you to gain access to the other planes. This exercise may stir up all kinds of fears and reactions, so be gentle on yourself for a couple of days afterwards. Discovering your death obviously involves looking into the future, and since much of the future is secret and guarded, it is important to have a clear intention, and to pray for assistance. For this purpose we call upon the Spirit of Death to help us.

Begin by lying down in a quiet place in the dark or low lighting and relax deeply. Taking a drop of Henbane flower essence, or burning a little dried Henbane will help you. Be aware of your intention to accept death, and then say the following prayer:

O Spirit of Death,
Thou who decides my final breath
Who awaits me at the end of life
To take me when the time is ripe
O ultimate power from which there is no escape
None can thwart thee, our ultimate fate
I surrender freely when my time is through
And worship thee and give thee the respect that is due
I ask thee now to help me see,
The time and way I shall come to thee

Let go of the physical plane and visualise yourself in the Void. The same spiral staircase that you used to walk down into your past lives now continues upwards before you. Walk up the staircase, realising that each step is one year, and carefully count the number of steps you take to reach the top. When you reach the top, just stop there and experience what it is like. You may not see the exact circumstances of your death because there will probably be some resistance to this, but you will have a feeling of what it is like to pass over. You now know the number of years until the time of your death. This knowledge often gives rise to a feeling of futility. Whatever the feeling, it is time to come to terms with it and to release your resistance. When you have experienced all there is to be found there, walk down the staircase back into the present. Thank the Spirit of Death, and return to normal life.

Exercise 8 - Astral Projection

There are several different methods of astral projection which take a good deal of time and energy to master. In this method, we enlist the help of tree spirits, which makes the process easier. A tree spirit is far more active than a human being can be on the Astral plane. You will be aware by this time of the importance of a well developed root to the process of our transition to inner planes. A tree is a being which has a root that is so well developed that it has become physically manifest. In a similar sense, a tree has no physical movement in this world because it embodies stillness. A tree's main actions are performed on the Astral plane. We can never have the mastery of the Astral plane that is native to trees because their line of evolution is different to ours. However, tree spirits can be great teachers and helpers for all our astral work and since working with tree spirits is always pleasant, and never seems to be an effort, you are likely to persist with this method of astral projection long enough to succeed.

Go into a wood and find a tree that feels friendly and make contact with it in the usual way. Once you have built a relationship with the tree, ask it to help you master astral projection. Then, just stand facing the tree and look at it for a while, with the intention of remembering exactly what it looks like. When you look at anything with the intention of memorising it, you begin to activate your astral eyes. This is because memory is a function that uses the astral plane, which, in turn, is closely related to the subconscious. Study the tree carefully for a few minutes, so that when you go away and close your eyes, you are able to picture it in detail. Practice this daily, so that in time you can visualise the tree in better and better detail.

The next step is to remember the feeling of being close by the tree. The feeling is more important than the sight, because it is through feeling that you make contact with the spirit of the tree. As you stand in front of the tree each day, be sensitive to how it feels, and learn to recall that feeling. Now when you close your eyes and imagine being in front of the tree, the spirit of the tree will be in contact with you, and some part of you will really be there.

Next, repeat the exercise using another nearby tree. In this way choose four or five trees in a row, and memorise each of them for a few minutes each day. What you are doing is setting up the path of your first out-of-body journey. When you can recall the sight and feel of each tree, just imagine yourself walking along this pathway each day, stopping before each tree, until one day you discover that you are actually there! Now the door is open for you to journey anywhere you like. Travel short distances at first, and gradually go further as you get a feel for it.

The value of this is that, not only can you travel in the physical world to see anything you need to see, but you can also travel out to meet the tree spirits and get to know them in a deeper way - even at night in your sleep.

Exercise 9 - Talking to Nature Spirits

A nature spirit once said to me "what you see limits you, what you cannot see sets you free". In this exercise we do not try to see nature spirits, or hear them, but we get to know them through their formlessness. They do not necessarily have form, nor do they speak in words, which means that to communicate with them we have to break out of our limited way of perceiving reality. This is very liberating to the spirit.

Go out into Nature, and let yourself be called to some spot. Do not look at physical things, or think about where to go, or why you are going there, just let yourself be called intuitively. When you arrive just be open to whatever messages come. Do not judge what is happening. You may think you are just imagining things, and that there is nothing really there, and that there is no reason for going to that particular place. In time, however, you will realise that there is great purpose in what is happening, and that you are able to have profound realisations. Practice will allow your intuition to develop in a very special way, so that eventually you will be able to perceive nature spirits all around, and develop an easy communication with them. You will find that there are many spirits that are willing to teach anyone who is capable of listening.

Exercise 10 - Extending Healing Energies

For this exercise root yourself as you did in the first tree spirit exercise. Bend your knees slightly and sink a little further, then round your shoulders slightly, so that there is a little space under your armpits, but keep the arms completely relaxed. You will feel a tingly feeling in the hands, as vital energy begins to flow through them. This energy can be used to heal and nourish the physical body, so get a feel for it. You can heal others by a simple laying on of hands, or by directing energy into acupuncture points. This, however, is only the lowest level of the healing energy. We need to understand the higher level which heals the emotions, mind and spirit.

The lower level of vital energy, which is known variously as chi, prana, animal magnetism and has many other names, bears a likeness to water in the way that it flows. The higher level of vital energy is more like fire, because it is faster and constantly renewing. Also, as it heals there can be a sensation of burning. This type of energy manifests as the kundalini or dragon fire. It has been said of dragon fire that when it meets water it increases and flares up. In other words, it is far more effective when the lower vital energy is also present. This is to be expected, since the physical level is the manifestation of the mental and spiritual spheres, and to heal one you must also heal the other.

Begin, therefore, by mastering the first level of vital energy. You can start to get a feel for the higher vital energy by visualising it as a violet flame. A flame is constantly renewing itself: it is never the same flame from second to second. This is the energy we need for being able to change and move on and not hold on to the past, or to traumas, old ties and mental blocks. Violet is the highest frequency of light in the visible spectrum, and therefore represents the highest vibration we can conceive. This vibration of vital energy gives rise to enthusiasm and unconditional love. We need to understand the importance of these qualities in healing. When we lack enthusiasm we begin to judge and suppress things, and become less able to handle life's challenges. Each time you make a judgement, you deny some aspect of life, and therefore deny a part of yourself, and so begin to suppress feelings. It is widely acknowledged that suppressed emotions are a major contribution to illness. You cannot help a person release feelings and blocks if you are judgmental because it was in reaction to this attitude that the person suppressed feelings in the first place.

What is needed is to accept people exactly as they are and not to feel that they should change. This is unconditional love. Instead of finding fault, you see a perfect, unique being who is creating its unique set of circumstances. Feel joy for such a marvellous creation and recognise that each person is a god, creating his/her environment perfectly, in accordance with the patterns of his/her inner consciousness. When you are able to have this attitude, there is no room for sympathy. Sympathy only resonates with the human creation of imperfection, not with the divine being within. Sympathy only encourages a person to wallow, not to release. When you totally accept a person and feel unconditional love and enthusiasm towards that person, your enthusiasm flows into them, raises their vibration and allows them to release their conditioning, and to release all blocks, and attachments to the past. The higher vital energy flows out to the person. When you look at people, learn to see the god within, let go of all judgement and try to radiate unconditional love and enthusiasm. Draw vital energy through your root, project it outwards as a violet flame, and see that flame as a vehicle for your enthusiasm and love. Feel how this increases the vibration of energy, until it actually seems to burn. Actually visualise the violet flame to begin with, but strive to get a feeling for the higher vibration so that you no longer need to rely on visualisation. By becoming conscious of the higher vital energy you will make it grow.

The higher vital energy or dragon fire comes from outside ourselves, and we must open to it through our spiritual devotion. It has been found that the pineal gland gives rise to enthusiasm. It is stimulated by natural sunlight, but not by artificial light, so the more time you spend outside in Nature, the more you will activate your pineal gland. Spiritual devotion will also activate it - so go out and be nourished by Nature, and inflame yourself with prayer. Also, give thanks to the Goddess for this divine gift, for gratitude opens the door for more.

VI

TECHNIQUES OF SHAMANIC HEALING

Since it is our consciousness that shapes our physical bodies, through the vehicle of our vital energy, healing needs to work on both the vital energy and the consciousness. Healing needs to include a number of processes: balancing and raising of vital energy; interpretation of symptoms to understand the emotional or mental cause; release of past traumas and conditioning, and, the infusion of positive energies. These processes are described in detail below.

Balancing and Raising Vital Energy

One of the most effective systems for balancing the vital energy involves the acupuncture meridians. This system is not exclusively Chinese; it was shared by early healers of many cultures, although the method of treatment varied. The reason why acupuncture became more popular than other methods is that it does not require the practitioner to master control of vital energy, the insertion of needles being sufficient. Its major limitation is that it can only rebalance those energies that are already present, it does not feed extra vital energy into the patient's system.

When you use our shamanic method, your first step is to root yourself and feel the flow of vital energy and then you direct energy through a finger into an acupuncture point, or use a healing wand with its resident tree spirit. This method has greater healing power because it not only balances, but renews and increases a patient's vital energy.

Some useful acupuncture points are described here, but I do not intend to spend much time on them since the main goal of our healing method is to change the consciousness of the person you are healing. If the consciousness does not change, the person will recreate the problem and the healing will not be permanent. The step of balancing and raising vital energy should not be left out, however, since all levels of being are interconnected, and if we are to make a change on a higher level, then the physical energies must be prepared also.

Muscle Testing

To balance these energies we need a method of diagnosis. If you have carried out the exercises given in the last chapter, you will be able to tune in to a patient and feel what needs to be done. However, until you develop this ability fully, you will find muscle tests useful for testing the state of energy in the meridian.

Basic Procedure

The next sections cover the fourteen meridians, their muscle tests, and some useful acupuncture points. Each muscle test is illustrated with a diagram. Learn the tests from the diagrams and from the descriptions given and then proceed as follows: ask the patient to hold the arm or leg in the position indicated in the diagram. Then ask him or her to resist your push against the limb and indicate in which direction you intend to push. If the muscle under test holds firm, the meridian is balanced. If it gives way, the meridian needs healing.

Fourteen Muscle Tests

The fourteen tests included here are sufficient for our purposes. More detailed descriptions of tests and points can be obtained from any good book about kinesiology and/or acupuncture.

Table 6.1 shows the fourteen meridians and the tests that apply to them.

Meridian	Test
Central	Supraspinatus
Governing	Teres Major
Stomach	Pectoralis Major Clavicular
Spleen/Pancreas	Latissimus Dorsi
Heart	Subscapularis
Small Intestine	Quadriceps
Bladder	Peroneus
Kidney	Psoas
Heart Governor/Circulation Sex	Gluteus Medius
Triple Warmer	Teres Minor
Gallbladder	Anterior Deltoid
Liver	Pectoralis Major Sternal
Lung	Serratus Anterior
Large Intestine	Fascia Lata

Table 6.1: Muscle Tests

Central Meridian

This meridian governs the Central Nervous System.

Muscle Test: *Supraspinatus*

Hold the arm about 15 degrees to the side of the body and slightly forward. Push in towards the centre line.

Acupuncture Points:

      i)   Top of the pubic bone
      ii)   Just below the tip of the sternum
      iii)   Top of the sternum
      iv)   In the dip between the chin and the lower lip

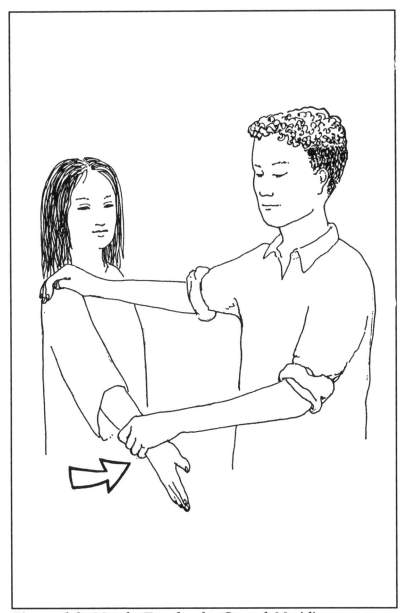

Figure 6-1: Muscle Test for the Central Meridian

Governing Meridian

This meridian governs the energy flow up the spine.

Muscle Test: *Teres Major*

Put the back of the hand into the small of the back, ask the patient to hold the elbow back. Try to push it forward.

Acupuncture Points:

> i)   On the spine in the small of the back
> ii) Centre at the base of the skull at the back
> iii) Between the nose and the upper lip

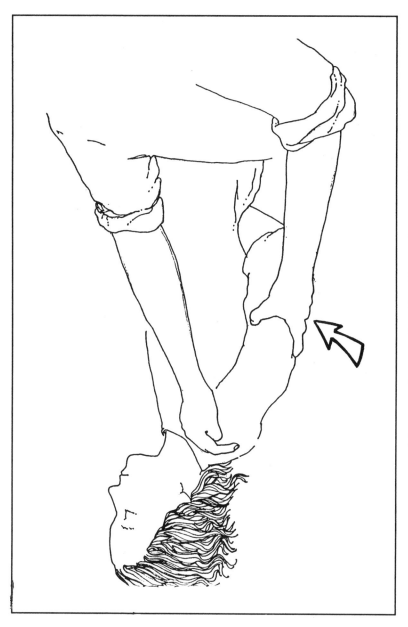

Figure 6-2: Muscle Test for the Governing Meridian

Stomach Meridian

Muscle Test: *Pectoralis Major Clavicular*

Hold the arm straight forward from the body, with the thumb downwards. Push down and out.

Acupuncture Points:

i)   One hand breadth beneath the knee, on the outer edge of the shin bone

ii)   On front of the ankle, in the slight dip between the two small tendons that show when the ankle is flexed

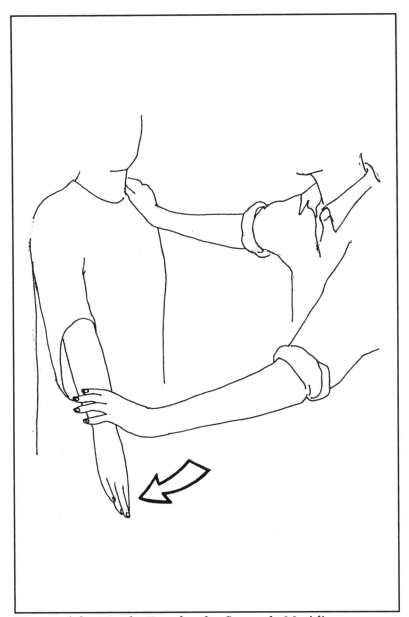

Figure 6-3: Muscle Test for the Stomach Meridian

Spleen/Pancreas Meridian

Muscle Test: *Latissimus Dorsi*

With the arm straight, turn the back of the hand against the body. Pull out away from the body.

Acupuncture Points:

      i)   On the inside of the foot, at the base of the big toe
      ii)   Inside of the foot, proximal to the bulge at the base of the big toe
      iii)   One hand width above the inner ankle bone

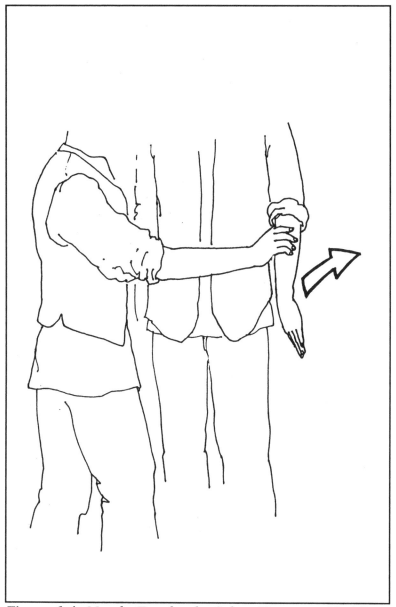

Figure 6-4: Muscle Test for the Spleen/Pancreas Meridian

Heart Meridian

Muscle Test: *Subscapularis*

Hold the upper arm out at right angles to the side of the body, with the elbow bent at right angles, so the hand points down the body. Try to lift the wrist.

Acupuncture Points:

      i)   On the fold of the wrist in line with the little finger
      ii)   On the little finger by the inner edge of the nail

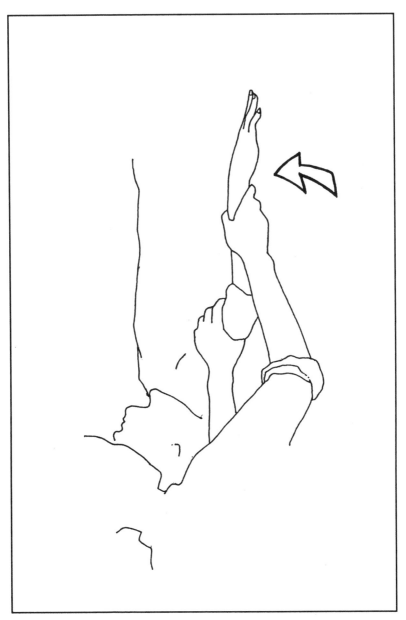

Figure 6-5: Muscle Test for the Heart Meridian

Small Intestine Meridian

Muscle Test: *Quadriceps*

Lift the knee until the thigh is at right angles to the body. Try to push it back down.

Acupuncture Points:

      i)   On the side of the hand at the base of the little finger

      ii)   On the little finger side of the wrist

      iii)   In the centre of the shoulder blade

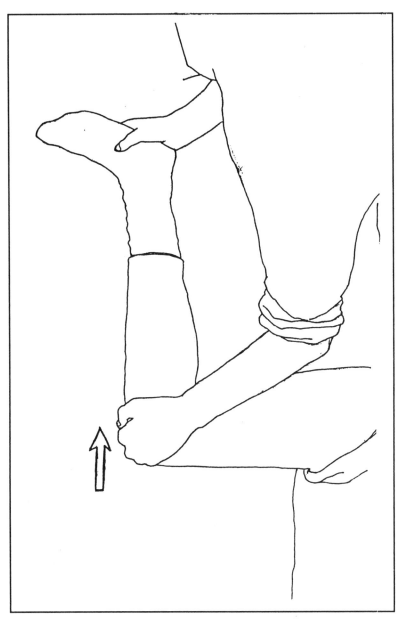

Figure 6-6: Muscle Test for the Small Intestine Meridian

Bladder Meridian

Muscle Test: *Peroneus*

Flex the ankle and turn the toes outwards.   Try to twist the toes inward.

Acupuncture Points:

     i)   Behind the outer ankle bone
    ii)   Just below the outer ankle bone
   iii)   On the little toe, on the outer corner of the nail

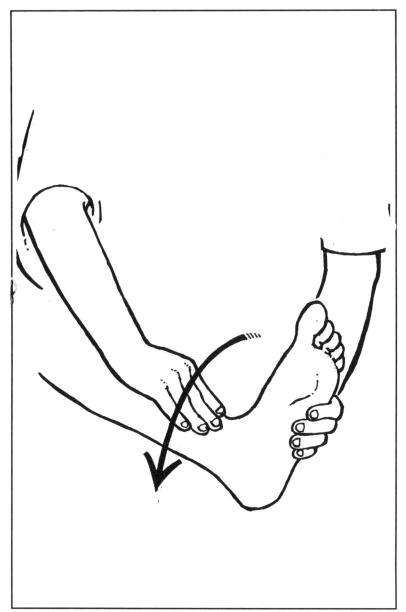

Figure 6-7: Muscle Test for the Bladder Meridian

Kidney Meridian

Muscle Test: *Psoas*

Lift the leg up straight with the foot turned outward. Push down and out.

Acupuncture Points:

     i)   Inside the foot, on the most concave part of the heel

     ii)   Two or three inches above the inner ankle bone, between the bone and the achilles tendon

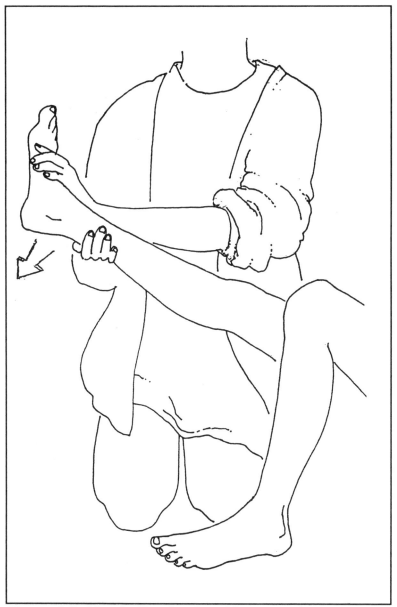

Figure 6-8: Muscle Test for the Kidney Meridian

Heart Governor or Circulation-Sex Meridian

Muscle Test: *Gluteus Medius*

Hold one leg to the side. Push towards other leg.

Acupuncture Points:

    i)   Inside of wrist, about 1 1/2 inches from fold

    ii)   On the palm of the hand, in the centre of the 'head' line

    iii)   On the middle finger, by the inner corner of the nail

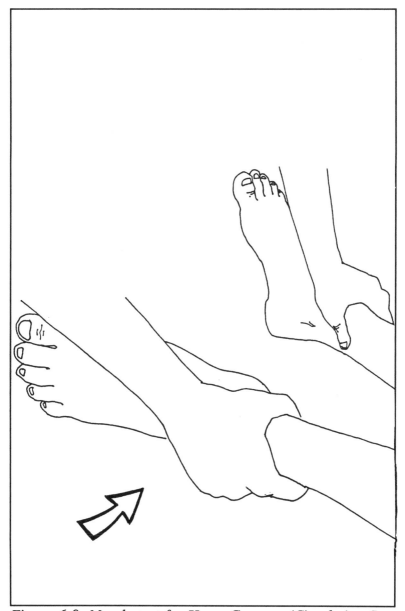

Figure 6-9: Muscle test for Heart Governor/Circulation-Sex Meridian

Triple Warmer Meridian

Muscle Test: *Teres Minor*

Hold the elbow close to the body, with the forearm turned outward. Push the forearm forward across the body.

Acupuncture Points:

    i)   On the back of the hand, between 4th and 5th metacarpals
    ii)   Back of wrist, between the two bones
    iii)   Just behind the tip of the elbow

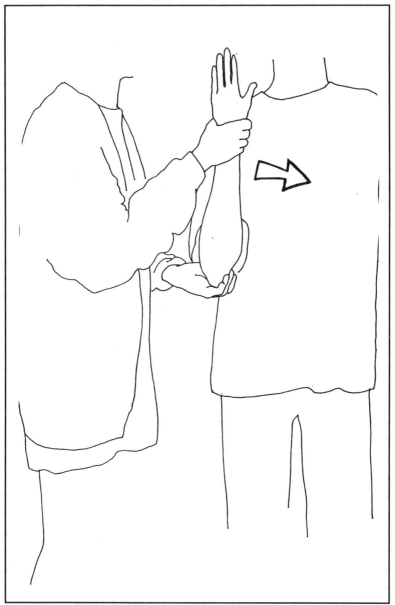

Figure 6-10: Muscle Test for the Triple Warmer Meridian

Gallbladder Meridian

Muscle Test: *Anterior Deltoid*

Hold the arm straight, 30 degrees forward from the body. Push back.

Acupuncture Points:

    i)   Base of the skull, an inch to either side of the centre
    ii)   Five finger breadths above the outer ankle bone
    iii)   On the instep, between the 4th and 5th metatersals

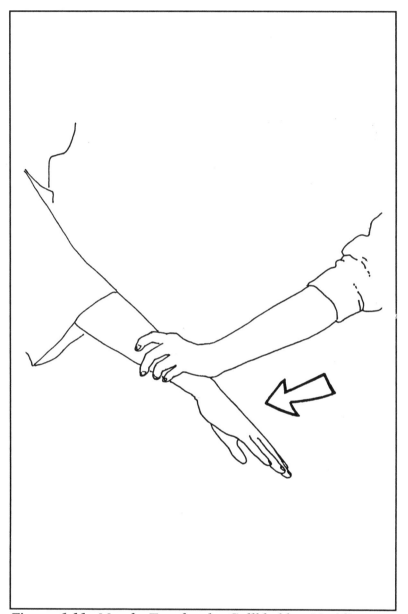

Figure 6-11: Muscle Test for the Gallbladder Meridian

Liver Meridian

Muscle Test: *Pectoralis Major Sternal*

Hold the arm straight forward at right angles to the body, with the thumb turned downwards. Push up and out.

Acupuncture Points:

i)   One inch above the big toe on the instep
ii)   Inside edge of the knee joint, on the most prominent part

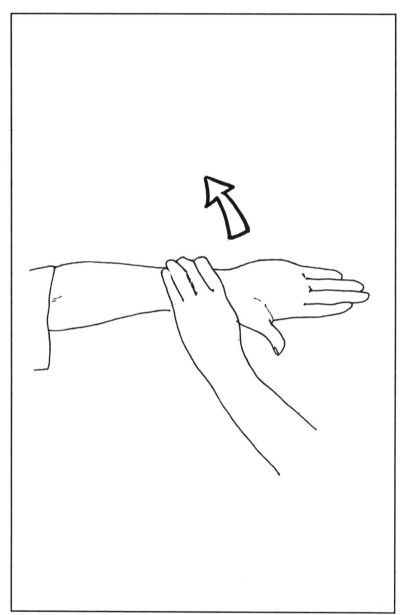

Figure 6-12: Muscle Test for the Liver Meridian

Lung Meridian

Muscle Test: *Serratus Anterior*

Hold the arm up high, brace the scapula, and pull the arm down.

Acupuncture Points:

i)   An inch below the centre of each collar bone
ii)   Inside the elbow joint on the radial side of the tendon
iii)   Inside the wrist at the point where the pulse is taken

Figure 13: Muscle Test for the Lung Meridian

Large Intestine Meridian

Muscle Test: *Fascia Lata*

With the toes turned inward, hold the leg up and out, and push towards the other leg.

Acupuncture Points:

    i)   On the back of the hand, where the bones meet between the thumb and forefinger

    ii)   On the back of the arm, near the elbow, just below a small bump on the head of the radius

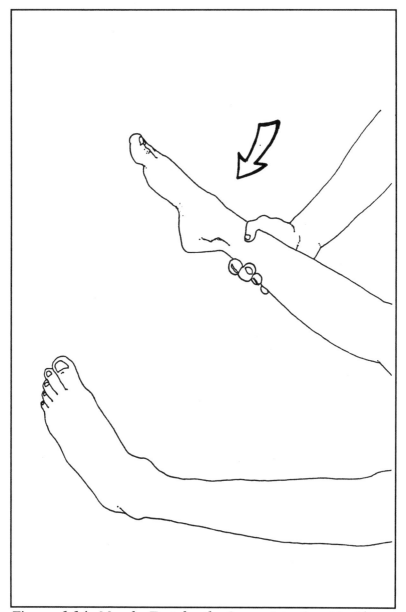

Figure 6-14: Muscle Test for the Large Intestine Meridian

Interpretation of Physical Imbalances

Moving to a deeper level of healing, our next step is to interpret any physical imbalances we find so that we can understand the patterns of consciousness that cause them. Chapter Two explains the relationship between physical imbalances and the patterns of consciousness that led to them. Use the information given there to find the underlying disturbances and then, to discover when they occurred, look at the inside edge of the patient's foot (see Figure 6-15). This part of the foot can be read as a time scale, showing our development from conception up to the present.

Note that there are four major changes in the curvature of this area of the foot. These changes in curvature correspond to important transitional periods in our life and indicate the times at which we are most impressionable. By taking note of where the curvature changes you can allocate the appropriate age range to the different sections of this part of the foot.

The first important transition occurs at the moment of conception. At this time the soul is first welcomed into incarnation. If the parents were not very positive at the time, or were unsure about having a baby, the soul probably did not feel secure about coming into incarnation, and, therefore, would have been born with a lack of trust in life. This can create a lot of tension throughout the life, damaging the gallbladder and possibly the heart.

The second critical time is the moment when the foetus divides into a head and a body about four weeks after conception. This is the time when the cranial-sacral pulse is established. This is the time, also, when the mother is most likely to discover she is pregnant. Any disturbance at this time can lead to the cranial and sacral pulses being unsynchronised, and the solar plexus, centred between the two, takes the strain. The person may be emotionally vulnerable all through life if these are the circumstances of early pregnancy.

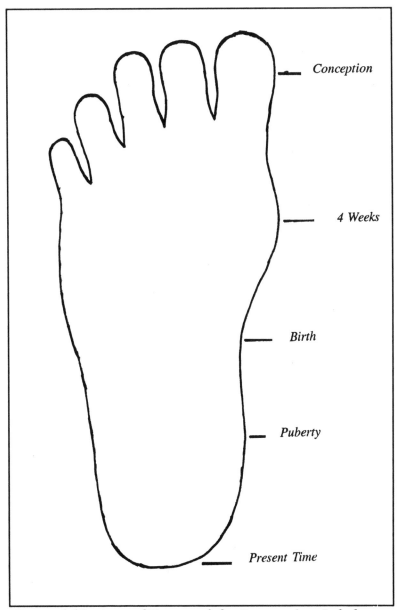

Figure 6-15: Area of Foot used for Interpreting Imbalances

The third impressionable period occurs at birth. The baby depends most on its mother's assistance to come through into the world. If the birth does not happen naturally and the baby is not pushed out normally, it will lose confidence firstly, in its own ability to succeed against life's challenges, and secondly, in any help that might come from others. This lack of confidence weakens the kidneys.

The fourth and final state of great impressionability occurs at puberty. The adolescent can be overwhelmed by a flood of new desires and feelings and by awakening to all the responsibilities adulthood will bring. There is a lot for the adolescent to come to terms with, and, if this is not understood by those dealing with the adolescent at this time, then he or she can suffer a great deal of worry. This worry can become a habit which will eventually damage the stomach. Often our education system puts even more stress on the adolescent at this already difficult time. The effects of these various stresses are stored and will show up as troubles later on.

A perfectly healthy foot should be smooth and evenly curved. Any traumas show as inconsistencies in the tissue at the appropriate point on the 'time scale' of the foot. There are three things to look for. Firstly, creases in the skin will show when mental blocks were formed. Secondly, patches of fluid under the skin show a build-up of suppressed emotion. Thirdly, changes in the bone structure of the foot show energy blocks that have distorted the body physically. Bunions are the most common example of this distortion. By their position you can see that a problem occurred during the fourth week after conception. The disturbed solar plexus affects the posture of a person, with hunched shoulders being the outward sign.

By this time, you should know how to find traumas and the approximate age at which they occurred in a patient. You can pinpoint the age more accurately by using the *opponens pollicis longus* muscle test. Ask the patient to hold the little finger against the thumb while you try to gently pull them apart (see Figure 6-16). Then, mention to the patient an age which is close to the approximate age you have previously diagnosed by looking at the foot. Perform the muscle test as you mention the age. Continue to try different ages, testing the muscle each time. The muscle will test weak i.e. the finger and thumb will separate, when you find the age at which the traumas occurred. You can use this method to find the exact date for each of the patient's traumas.

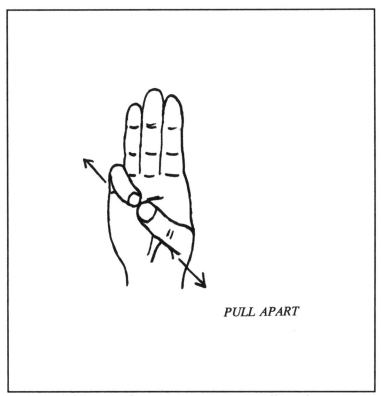

PULL APART

Figure 6-16: Muscle Test - opponens pollicis longus

Releasing Traumas and Conditioning

In order to release a trauma that occurred in the current life or in a past life, the patient has to re-experience it fully, consciously, and without resistance. The technique we use for this is Regression. The energy needed to work through the block and rise above it comes from the higher vital energy which you will have to project into the patient during the regression process.

Current Life Regression

It is important that the patient is relaxed and rooted so that he or she can let go fully. If the patient is tense, you can take him/her through a relaxation process which allows the strength you have from your own root to help the patient. To begin with, therefore, root yourself and hold the patient's feet, gently but firmly. Ask the patient to relax. As you guide the relaxation process, starting with the feet and from there up the body, hold each part of the body in turn, whilst keeping yourself rooted. The patient will feel safely held and, therefore, will be able to let go more easily.

As you begin the regression process, you will need to extend your higher vital energy into the patient. If you do not yet have a feel for this, simply visualise a violet flame and keep your enthusiasm high. You can either put your hand on the organ that needs healing most, or hold the appropriate acupuncture point, or lightly hold the patient's forehead to activate the front brain. This restores choice, and will help release the 'reactiveness' of the mental block.

Here is an example of the type of induction you will need to regress a patient. Let us assume that you have found a trauma at four years old.

> *"Just relax and let go. Let all your body go limp, and just sink onto the bench.· Allow all the cares of the day to just drift away, so for the time being nothing outside this room*

matters. Just relax and let go. Forget about the world, and think only of the darkness and emptiness of space, as if you are out in the Void. As I guide you back, there is no need to strain to see anything, just relax and let go, and allow any feelings or memories to arise naturally. You are going to follow me backwards in your imagination. As you relax, out in the Void, below you is large spiral staircase, which winds down and down into the darkness. Begin to walk down this staircase, realising that each step is one year, so as you go down, you are going further and further back in time. Just continue down at your own pace, gradually going further and further into the past. You are going down through time, through your childhood, back to the age of four. I am going to count down from ten to zero, and when I reach zero, you will be at the age of four".

Then count down from ten to zero, pause a moment, then say to the patient: "how do you feel?". Encourage the patient to re-live the whole trauma in full, as if it were happening right then, at that moment. Whatever the feeling, whether it's anger, fear, shock, grief, pain or a whole range of different feelings, ask the patient to feel fully, and to intensify the feeling(s), and to be enthusiastic about the process. You will feel great energy changes in your hands at this time. When the patient has finished, ask him or her to re-live the experience once more, but this time to realise that the whole thing is his or her own creation, and, therefore, quite illusory. Explain to the patient that he or she is simply going to experience the event this second time as if in a theatre, and, just like being in a theatre, he or she can get emotionally involved. Ask the patient to tell you when this experience has finished. Now, since the event is the patient's own creation, then the patient can change it. The patient still has free choice, and is capable of creating a happy ending. Ask the patient to imagine the situation resolving with the best possible outcome for him or herself. Ask the patient to tell you when this is finished. End by asking the patient to leave the situation behind now, and to climb back up the spiral staircase to the present, as you count up from zero to ten.

Infusing a Positive Pattern

Creating a positive ending to the experience, as described above, is one way of bringing in a positive pattern. We need other ways of doing this as well because people are highly individual and vary in their needs. In the case of a childhood trauma, which occurred when the child was needing love or support, it is often better to ask the patient to go back in time to support the inner child. The adult, as he or she is now, is able to replace an unloving parent, to give the child whatever it needs and to talk to it to make it feel better.   This is rather important where childhood traumas are concerned, because a small child is generally self-centred and takes everything personally. It can feel unworthy if it is deprived, and can feel it is to blame if the parents are fighting etc. It is good to reassure the child therefore. The adult can be quite free in giving the child what it needs to feel loved and confident. This can include anything, like giving it the extra pocket money it wants, or "beating up" a bullying neighbour. (In the imagination, of course!) The process can finish with the patient giving his or her inner child an appropriate gemstone, as a gift, to bring in a quality that was lacking. Some useful gemstones include: Golden topaz - to restore self-worth; Fire Opal - to restore creativity; Emerald - to restore a sense of connectedness, to other people or to the feelings; Amethyst - to restore self-love; Lapis Lazuli - to give a sense of equality; Ruby - to restore originality and, finally, Herkimer Diamond - to restore faith.

Flowers or flower essences are also extremely useful. They can be used during or after the regression. If you feel a particular flower is appropriate to help release the trauma you are working on, place either the fresh flower or a bottle of flower essence on the patient's body, on whichever chakra is most involved, and leave it there during the whole regression process. On the other hand, after a regression you may feel a flower essence is needed to reinforce a positive view of life, or to help the patient grow out of old habits. Again, place the flower or flower essence on the body on the appropriate chakra. Hold your hand two to two and a half feet above the surface of the body and you will feel a layer of energy, formed by the interaction of the flower energy with the patient's chakra. As you allow energy to flow from your hand (or you can use a live wand), this layer of energy will slowly move down. Follow it until your hand reaches the surface of the body. The flower essence will now be fully integrated into the chakra.

Alternatively, you can give the patient a flower essence as a remedy to take for some days following the healing session.

Past Life Regression

Sometimes, when working with a patient, you can find patterns which do not disappear if you deal only with the traumas of his or her current life. Quite often the situations a patient has trouble with are blown out of proportion because he or she has karma with other individuals, i.e. the reaction a person has to a situation cannot be justified until you look at past life links with the people involved. The same regression process we have just looked at can be used to take a person into previous incarnations.

The process for regressing to past lives varies slightly, because we have no way of selecting an exact regression time. Instead we have to be guided by the particular pattern the patient is working with. For example, suppose we have a patient whose problems have been found to stem from the very disempowering effect his mother has had on him. The patient seems to have been born with this problem and there is no indication of a specific time when the problems started. In the induction you would say something like this:

"You continue down through time, beyond this life, through the darkness between lives, back towards the life in which this pattern with your mother began. As you go down through time, you feel that life-time getting closer, until gradually it unfolds before you. I am going to count down from ten to zero, and when I reach zero, you will be at that life-time when the karma with your mother began".

The rest of the process then continues in the same way as that described before. You ask the patient to re-live the experience, then bring in something positive, and finally you ask the patient to return, up the staircase and into the present.

You need to use discrimination to decide when it is more appropriate to regress a patient to a past life rather than working through traumas from the current life. Some people like to play the victim, and to take such a person back to previous incarnations to see what other awful things have been done to him or to her will only reinforce a victim status. This is, of course, quite detrimental. It is better to help the patient to deal with his or her current problems before uncovering new ones. Victim patterns need to be cleared first. These nearly always stem from childhood, because it is when we are small children that we really are helpless, and, therefore, become victims. There is no point in taking a person through any experience that he or she is unwilling to lovingly endure and take responsibility for, and as much encouragement as possible should be given in this direction.

Psychic Healing

When you are healing and changing a person's consciousness, it is also necessary to take the astral body into account. In any traumatic experience which involves other people, there is a certain energy exchange, and healing can be helped by dealing with these energy exchanges on the astral plane. These exchanges between people can be seen as threads of energy connecting people together. These threads are 'aka cords'. Energy flows down this cord and both parties are affected. Whenever someone has "put you down" or disempowered you in some way, that person has taken something from you. Your energy will be flowing down the aka cord, keeping you weak. In order to fully heal the trauma, you need to cut the cord and take your energy back.

It is interesting to look at the number of aka cords you carry from past lives, and how these can cause you to lose out to others in various different current life situations. The cords particularly affect your success in love, because they can take away your personal magnetism. Cutting these cords and taking back your power not only heals you physically and emotionally, it can change your whole destiny.

There are two plant helpers that are very useful for this particular work. Belladonna is the plant that destroys aka cords, and Marjoram is the plant for calling back power that has been taken away. You can work with these either by journeying to the Underworld to gain them as allies, or by keeping bottles of the flower essences at your side. In practice, the power of these plants can be invoked through sound vibrations, which can be made with your voice. Belladonna responds to a high-pitched sound, Marjoram responds to a low intonation.

At first you will be able to see the aka cords best in the Underworld. When you find them, just take a knife and cut them. The knife obviously needs to be built into your Underworld and consecrated for this purpose. Prepare a live-wood knife and ask the tree spirit to help you. Once the cords are cut, call back your power, allowing the Marjoram to help you, and then take your power back with you when you leave the Underworld.

When doing this work with a patient, it can be included in the regression process. The patient will be in a trance state already and will be ready to see aka cords when asked to look for them. When the patient has re-lived a trauma, ask him or her to look in a mirror and see if there are any cords attached to the body. The cords will usually be attached to major chakras. When the patient finds a cord, ask what percentage of his or her energy is flowing down it. Then ask the patient to visualise a knife, a pair of scissors or a sword, whatever feels most appropriate, and cut the cord. As the patient does this, make a high-pitched sound to invoke the Belladonna. (The patient will not need a pre-prepared knife if you are working with Belladonna.) Finally, ask the patient to call back all his or her energy, as you make a low intonation to invoke the Marjoram spirit.

Psychic Attack

Although genuine psychic attack is very rare, many people are vulnerable to the negative thoughts of others. At some point you will need to deal with psychic attack, whether it is a deliberate attack by a trained occultist, or simply 'bad vibes' from negative people. Rather than getting involved in any drawn-out psychic battle, you would do better to remember that everything you experience in life is your own creation. If somebody is attacking you, it is your consciousness that has drawn that person into your life. To stop a patient suffering from attack, the cause, within the patient's own consciousness, must be healed first.

There are several reasons why psychic attack experiences are drawn to us:

1 A victim complex. In states of grief, it is difficult to maintain self-responsibility and not to blame your troubles on the outer world. This can develop into a deep-seated belief that something in the world is out to harm you. With this belief, you are going to manifest harmful energies.

2 Guilt. This leads to a hidden wish for self-punishment, which the subconscious mind will tend to oblige. There are basically three kinds of guilt. Firstly, there is actual guilt because you have intentionally harmed others. In this case, you should try to make amends, and learn to forgive

yourself as you forgive others. Secondly, there is a sense of unworthiness, when you believe you should have done better and cannot forgive yourself for not meeting the high standards you set for yourself. This state is actually a form of arrogance, because you lack the humility to accept your imperfections. Thirdly, guilt can result from religious conditioning. This is the most unnecessary guilt of all, conditioned into you by false teachers who wish to manipulate everyone. Change this conditioning by re-reading Chapter 1: "Fundamental Principles".

3   Hate, or a wish to harm others. The subconscious does not discriminate between self and others. Whatever you wish on others, the subconscious believes the same is right for you. If you wish harm on others, the subconscious will manifest something harmful to you.

Hate is not the same as anger. Aggression can be positive. It is sometimes needed to clear whatever blocks the way, either to getting things done, or to following your true will. The wish to harm others is not inherent in anger. But hate arises when aggression is suppressed through fear. Usually this is fear of disapproval. This type of fear arises when you place anybody in a position of authority above yourself. Similarly, guilt is conditioned into us when we bow down to authority. This subservience to authority is due to a lack of self-knowledge. The victim complex also arises because we do not recognize our true creative selves. So - the ultimate answer to all these problems is self-realisation, which will, in turn, make us immune to any form of psychic attack.

To help you along the way, and keep you on the correct path, read the following affirmation regularly:

> *"We are all gods, creating our bodies and our environments perfectly according to the patterns of our consciousness. Anybody else in our lives was drawn there by our consciousness and simply fulfils the role in our lives that our consciousness has dictated. We can create unconsciously, or we can choose to take conscious control of what we create. We can also choose not to choose. That too is our choice".*

Choosing to change is obviously a long term work. If you have to deal with a psychic attack as an emergency, the first thing to do is to use the purification and banishing ritual given in Chapter Five. This will dispel any harmful energies. You should then work on clearing any grief, victim complexes, guilt or hate, by using the therapies already described in this chapter.

Dealing with Possession

It is quite common for a person's problems to be aggravated by some other being that has entered the Aura. The only way an external intelligence can gain any degree of control is if we give up our self-governance. Losing self-governance means relinquishing consciousness, or losing consciousness. This is not the same as the loss of consciousness that occurs during sleep. One does not lose self-governance whilst asleep, because sleep is a natural process which does not involve any loss of self. Any other time consciousness is lost, through alcohol, drugs, anaesthetics, hypnosis or trauma, an opening is created in the Aura, and since Nature abhors a vacuum, something will come to fill the gap. Whatever astral entities are in the vicinity of the unconscious person will go into the Aura. These may be thought-forms of others that have been created by a powerful emotional event, or they may be discarnate human souls that have not passed on from this plane. It is even possible for animal spirits that are still attached to this world to enter the Aura.

You can become aware of possession when, for instance,

after an operation you find yourself having thoughts that you did not have before. People who take drugs or alcohol are particularly prone to possession by the souls of other addicts. When drug addicts or alcoholics pass away, their level of consciousness is usually not evolved enough to be able to let go of the material world; they are still seeking a 'fix', but cannot experience the effect except through the physical body of another addict. Since it is likely that the discarnate souls will continue to frequent the places where they indulged their habits whilst alive, it will be easy for these souls to enter the bodies of fellow addicts who also use these places regularly. In this way an alcoholic or drug addict compounds his or her condition by adding to it the problem of possession.

Simply casting out the entities from a person does not solve the problem. If the hole in the Aura is not healed and remains open, something else will fill it. So we must concentrate on healing the hole in the Aura by encouraging the patient to work through the unconsciousness that is stored there. This unconsciousness will be experienced in the body as numbness, and in the mind as a light-headed, floaty feeling. The patient must lovingly endure these sensations and remain conscious throughout the experience. Possessing entities are naturally squeezed out in the process, and can be felt as a cold wind leaving the body.

The method of treatment varies according to the cause of the possession. In the cases of trauma or operation, we can use the regression process to take the patient back to the time of the trauma or operation. In these cases, we can help trigger the memory by pressing the painful part of the body involved in the trauma. For an operation, for example, we can hold the painful spot on the operation scar, and direct higher vital energy into it. If there has been injury, we can press any painful spot on the injured part of the body, and direct violet flame or higher vital energy into it. Pressing the spine is particularly good for this type of work, as the energy flow up the spine plays an important role in generating the Aura. Any holes in the Aura will have corresponding lesions on the spine. When you guide a patient back to the time of a trauma, he or she will feel numb and floaty. When the cold winds have passed and the numbness has worn off, bring the patient back.

If hypnosis is the cause of possession, then, in addition to the unconsciousness, there will be an aka cord to the hypnotist because the patient has given up power to the hypnotist. This connection is easily released by cutting the cord and taking back power from the hypnotist. Invoking Belladonna will also help cast out the entity.

Drug addicts and alcoholics are more difficult to deal with. Since there is a gradual weakening in the patient due to a long period of regular abuse, regression to release a specific trauma, at a particular point in time, is not possible. We can trigger the release of unconsciousness through the body by pressing painful points as described before. In this case we should press the gonad reflex points. All unconscious experiences build up in the gonads (prostate and testicle for men, ovaries and uterus for women).

Prior to point-holding the patient must build up the body nutritionally. A raw food diet and the addition of minerals before the healing session will create the conditions needed for change to take place within the body. The healing session may take a few hours.

The gonad reflex points are on either side of the heel, close to the ankle. Find the painful spots on both sides, just below and slightly behind the inner and outer ankle bones, and squeeze them together. Flood the whole of the patient's body with higher vital energy. The patient will become numb and light-headed. Encourage the patient to experience this consciously, and make sure that he or she does not black out. You may have to talk to the patient and prod a bit to keep him or her awake. During this process the points you are pressing can become hot and your fingers may burn, or else your fingers may just feel very numb. When this stage is over, the points will pulse for a while; when the pulsing stops the process is over. Whilst the points are being held you may feel cold winds emanate from the patient several times;

these signify the release of entities. As possessing entities are squeezed out of the Aura, it is good to help them leave this plane, so they are not left hanging around. Remember that such entities are often lost human or animal souls which need help to get free. When you feel an entity leaving the body, command it in the name of the Goddess (or whatever gods you believe in) to leave this plane and continue its evolution elsewhere. Then ask the Angel of Death, Azariel, to guide it across the threshold.

Here is an invocation I have written for freeing trapped souls; I have found it useful for the processes described here and, also, for curing cases of haunting:

"O Great Goddess, who gives all their rightful place
Let thy power now fill this space
We have need of thee to release a soul
Who is trapped, unable to fulfil its goal.
We pray to thee to show thy might
And clear the illusions that block his sight
So that he may see his true path ahead
And fully pass from the living to the dead
It was thee that brought him into birth
And gave him a place upon this Earth
It was thee that gave him his every breath
Send him now the angel of Death
Mighty Azariel, Great Angel, help him across
Let him see that there is really no loss
Release him from this plane, help him to let go
Deliver him to the Goddess, so he may know
His next step towards his destiny
From his Earthly chains he must now be free
O Great Goddess, as you send all to their rightful place
Let harmony rule within this space

By the power of the Goddess I set thee free
With love I wish to help you see

Your way ahead, beyond this plane
I command you to leave your mortal frame
And speed across to the other side
With the Angel Azariel at your side
Your time here is ended, do not stay
My blessings go with you on your way

Entities can also be released through Underworld workings, but this cannot be taught in a book. As you gain more experience of shamanic journeying, you will find your own ways of doing this.

Healing Group Elementals

Whenever two or more people get together for a common purpose, there is always a blending of elemental energies to some degree. This leads to the formation of a group elemental which has a separate existence from the people in the group and yet, at the same time, influences each individual in the group to keep them aligned with its purpose. A good example of this is the case of mob violence, when people do things together that normally no individual alone would dream of doing. In this situation the group elemental takes over and it follows its autonomous purpose. All groups and societies form group elementals. You may find that when dealing with groups it is very difficult to make any kind of reform, or even have any real communication, because the individual intelligences are limited by the group elemental which can only maintain its original purpose. To effect a change you would do far better to look beyond the individuals and project your thoughts into the group elemental. If you have been a part of any organisation, you will need to be aware of this principle, so that you can free yourself and maintain your own will and power. By being aware of the group elemental, you can consciously separate from it and take back your power.

There is one particular kind of group elemental which we need to consider: this is the elemental of a marriage or a relationship between two people. All marriages involve a third entity, and the success of the marriage depends very much upon this marriage elemental. Even as people can suffer the effects of negative thoughts, so too can the relationship elemental. Often, the two individuals are quite healthy and balanced and are not under any direct attack, but jealousy towards the relationship from another quarter weakens the elemental. In the end the relationship fails for no obvious reason. Many relationships which have great potential fail in this way, because the state of the elemental has not been taken into account. The relationship elemental can also have aka cords and scars dating from past lives. A couple may have a strong link from previous incarnations, and are very strongly drawn together, and yet the relationship may be doomed to failure from the beginning because of the karmic weaknesses and the old aka cords the elemental is carrying. So you can see that a new angle of thinking is needed here; apart from healing the individuals, the relationship elemental must also be given healing as a separate entity.

Usual methods of healing are useless in this situation mainly because you cannot focus on a physical body since the elemental cannot normally be seen. However, you will be able to see it in the Underworld. The difficulty lies in recognising it.

For this work we need another plant ally: the Vipers Bugloss. This plant is particularly good for healing relationship elementals, and it will also guide you to them in the Underworld. When you find the relationship elemental the first thing to do is to cut all the ties that you can see, except for the two which connect it to the couple it belongs to. Then, call back any power that has been taken from it. This is the same process as described earlier, but this time use Vipers Bugloss instead of Marjoram. You cannot counsel or regress the elemental as if it were an actual person, but you can work on it in the Underworld, and give it flower essences to heal its psychic scars. You can simply remove any negative energies attached to it. Use either your higher vital energy or some ally to transmute such energies, or, send them back to where they came from. Give basic energy healing to any scars, and fill the elemental with Vipers Bugloss essence. You will find these techniques very useful for mending relationships and strengthening the bond of love. The couple can then be given a bottle of Vipers Bugloss flower essence to take together. It will be particularly powerful if taken during Tantra.

Advanced Healing Methods

The methods I describe here involve shamanic trance states, which can only be practised when you have gained a fair amount of experience of journeying to the Underworld, the Upperworld and to the Divine Essence. Once you have learned to journey into your own unconscious, you can then proceed to journey into another person's unconscious. This is very useful if for some reason he/she is unable to cooperate with you in the healing process; the patient can just lie still while you do all the inner work on his or her behalf. This help should only be given in the early stages of healing, however, because a person will never be empowered or become self-responsible, if he or she makes no effort towards his or her own healing. There are three techniques you can use: fetching a power animal, soul retrieval and guiding the person to the Divine Essence.

Fetching a Power Animal

The first thing you can do to bring strength to a weakened person is to bring them a power animal. When you decide to do this for someone remember to take your own allies with you as you journey down the tunnel beneath the patient into his or her Underworld, because you do not know yet what difficulties you might encounter. Once you are in the Underworld, search for a power animal, when you find one willing to come with you, take hold of it and carry it back up the tunnel. You will be holding the patient's power animal spirit in your hands when you arrive back, so immediately place your hands on the patient's chest and using your breath and a strong intention, blow the spirit into the chest of the patient.

Soul Retrieval

Another very useful practice is Soul Retrieval. Sometimes, a person is left in a coma following a trauma because the soul left the body. Finding the soul and blowing it back into the body can bring the person out of the coma. However, the shock and stress will still need to be dealt with. This is the classic model of total soul loss. Partial soul loss is far more common. There are several ways in which it can occur. A person may partly leave the body during trauma, in order to escape. The person is left in an empty state, often quite emotionless, and feeling incomplete. It is also possible to leave part of oneself with the other person when a deep relationship comes to an end. The third type of soul loss occurs when a part of the soul is stolen by an astral entity. This sounds strange, but is more common than you would expect. Entities often play a role in childhood illnesses. For the first three years of life, a child does not have its own Aura, but needs to be within its parents' Aura for safety. When alone, the child is very vulnerable and can be preyed upon by these disease entities. Often, after a severe illness the personality of the child changes because part of the soul is missing. These different types of soul loss are characterised by the feeling of not being quite complete.

To find a lost soul, or part of a soul, you need to be experienced at journeying in both the Underworld and the Upperworld, as well as being able to project in the physical plane. A lost soul can be on either plane and it is very difficult to search it out if you do not know where to start looking. Often, a thread can be found, attaching the soul to the body, and you can follow this thread to find the soul. In many cases soul retrieval is extremely difficult without a guide to lead you to the soul. The Cuckoo Pint is a very useful plant ally to use here. The astral body of the Cuckoo Pint tends to be separated from its physical body, and it has great freedom over all the inner planes. If you gain this plant as an ally, wherever the soul you are looking for happens to be the plant spirit can easily take you to it. Then, having found the soul, you can usually carry it back up the tunnel and return it to the person, but sometimes there are complications. It may be that the soul was stolen by an entity, and this entity still has possession of it. In this case you will have a fight on your hands to win back the soul. You will need the aid here of a guardian spirit such as the Destroying Angel, which is another very useful plant ally to use against entities. It is a small, white, sweet smelling mushroom that is extremely poisonous, so be careful how you make contact with it. Its spirit is very powerful, and I have never known an entity that could resist it. With this ally you will have no trouble in winning back the soul.

Another difficulty might arise if the soul you find is conscious enough to choose not to come back. Often the soul does not want to face the trauma that occurred to the body, and so will stay lost in the Astral, unwilling to come back. In this case you will have to speak to the soul for a while, reassuring it that healing is at hand, and pointing out that being lost in the Astral is a waste and that it cannot remain there forever. You can also feed flower energies to the soul to begin its healing before bringing it back to the body, and to help to give it courage and the will to live. Borage, Oak and Solomon's Seal are useful here. It is worth gaining the help of a large number of plant allies to prepare you for this kind of work.

Having found the soul and persuaded it to return, all that remains is to carry it back up the tunnel and blow it into the patient's body, in the same way as you did with power animals.

If you have not yet gained the right allies to fight off entities, remember that you can always journey to the Divine Essence, and bring back some divine energy to use in the Underworld. This is the highest and purest energy, and will overcome all obstacles. Later, you should also guide your patient to this essence, to empower and release blockages.

Guiding Patients to the Divine Essence

There are three tools you will need for this process: a drum and two rattles. One rattle is filled with small stones and the other is filled with seeds. The seeds represent new life, so this rattle is good for renewing energy. The stones represent the Earth, and this rattle is good for bringing things up from the Underworld, or bringing deep suppressions up to the surface.

Take patients into this work gradually, first getting them accustomed to the Underworld, then to the Upperworld, and then to the Divine Essence. Begin by asking the patient to relax. Use the same relaxation procedure as that described for Regression, holding each part of the body as the patient releases all tension. Patients need to relax more deeply in this work, so go a stage further by asking the patient to breathe slowly and deeply, in through the nose and out through the mouth. If you breathe with the patient you will be able to guide him or her into deeper relaxation. After a while ask the patient to breathe normally again, and to visualise some peaceful spot in Nature. Get the patient to go into great detail with this visualisation so that it gradually takes him or her away from the physical world and into inner worlds. Then ask the patient to find a hole in the ground that leads deep down into the Underworld. When the patient has found and described the hole to you, ask him or her to climb down into it and continue to journey deeper and deeper down this passage. Begin the drumbeat, and continue drumming throughout the whole process of journeying.

Let the patient indicate when he or she has reached the Underworld, and then guide him or her deeper, back beyond the time when the Earth had its beginning, until the patient finds himself or herself in the Upperworld. Continue to go back to the time before the beginning of the universe, until the patient finds himself or herself at the Divine Essence. There will be no visual image or sound here, because it is beyond anything the mind can conceive, just a great feeling of empowerment. Stop the drumbeat for a while, so that the patient can quietly experience the divine energy. You can use sacred sound here as an aid; use a kind of "Paaahh", huffing sound, not intoned, but made on the breath. Ask the patient to completely absorb the divine energy, and when the soul is filled the patient can begin the journey forward in time, through the Universe, towards the Earth and back to the body. The patient could go to the Underworld at this stage and use the divine energy to make some change there, but I will describe a slightly different process. When the person's soul returns from the Divine Essence and finds the Earth, rather than the Underworld, ask him or her to find the body, lying on the ground where it was left, and to look at it from above. In this state the person will be able to perceive any blocks in the body, and use the newly acquired divine energy to release them. (You will have to go through this process yourself to understand what it is like.) When the patient finds a blockage, which may consist of suppressed emotions, or may be an entity, or some other kind of negative energy, ask him or her to apply divine energy to intensify the blockage and build it up to the surface of the body. Use the stone rattle during this process. When the blockage has reached the surface, ask the patient to open up the Aura or 'psychic skin' over it, and then begin to push out all the negative energies. Tell the patient that these energies will be taken away and use the seed rattle. You will have to invoke your guardian spirits to help at this stage, or use the banishing ritual, or invoke whichever gods you believe in. You must make sure, however, that you have complete trust that the negative energies which are being released will be taken away by the spirits whom you have invoked. When the blockage is clear, ask the patient to fill the space that is left with divine energy, and then close the Aura. The patient may continue the procedure and remove other blocks if he or she wishes. When the patient has finished clearing blocks, ask him or her to realign himself or herself with the body. Next, to find himself or herself back in the tunnel which was used in the journey down, and then to begin to journey back up to the top. Use the drumbeat again to complete the journey. When the patient has reached the top, ask him or her what the year is, to confirm that the person is fully in the present. The patient has been in a deep trance and you should bring him or her back to normal slowly, by gently massaging the body.

VII

THE THIRTEEN SACRED TREES

There are thirteen trees in England which have always been revered as sacred. Their cycle is associated with the Moon so that each tree is at its most active, and guards the threshold, at a different full moon. The order in which the trees rotate through the cycle is: Birch, Rowan, Ash, Alder, Willow, Whitethorn, Oak, Holly, Hazel, Apple, Blackthorn, Elder and Yew. Some of the popular Celtic tree calendars try to fit the tree cycle to the solar year - but trees do not conform to human dogma, they follow their own rhythms. Since a thirteen moon cycle will not fit into our twelve month calendar, each year will be different. I can give you guidelines, but you will have to be in touch with the trees to sense the exact phases and become aware of how they really change.

Generally the first full moon of the New Year is ruled by the Birch. The Rowan is only ruling every third year, so some years will only have twelve tree-moons.

The phases of the tree year correspond to the stages of our lives, from conception to death, and the qualities we need to develop at each stage are those that can be received from the tree energies either in meditation or through healing practices. There are different protective trees for different stages of development. Familiarity with the characteristics of the thirteen trees, therefore, can give us great insight into human needs and the development of the psyche, and can provide powerful tools for healing and evolution.

You can identify the different trees using the illustrations of leaves, flowers and berries shown in Figures 7-1 and 7-2.

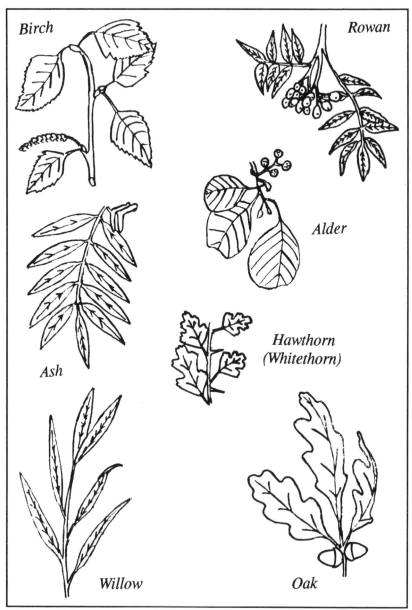

Figure 7-1: Leaves and Berries

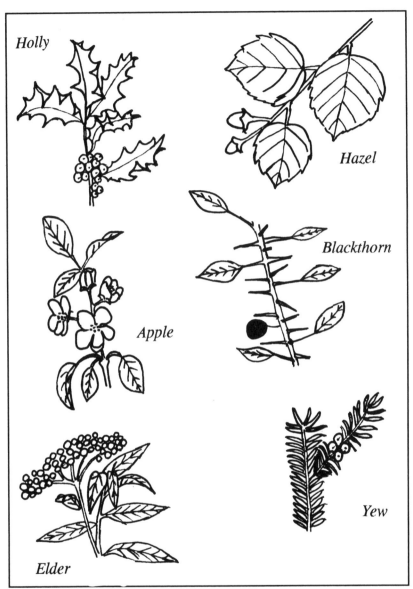

Figure 7-2: Leaves and Berries (cont)

Birch

Birch is the tree of conception and fertility. Its energy suggests limitless potential, and a continuous flow of new ideas and creative genius. Its moon is normally around the time of the Winter Solstice, when the Sun is reborn. It represents, therefore, the starting point of any new cycle or new project. A person's ability to produce new ideas, i.e. to bring things through from the creative source, depends upon the nature of his or her own entry into this plane of existence. If a soul does not feel welcome at the moment of conception, its creative genius is going to be limited. This can lead to a lack of self-confidence in a person. Physically, it will lessen fertility. Regression work can release the trauma of an unwelcoming entry into life, but it may not, necessarily, restore that connection with the source and creative genius which the soul should have gained already. Working with Birch tree spirits can bring in this quality when it is lacking.

The tree generally rules over most of the pregnancy period.

Rowan

Rowan is the tree of quickening, that stage of pregnancy where the baby is being prepared for birth. Its qualities ensure that creative ideas that result from the connection with the source are given that further impulse which brings them into material creation. This stage always needs an extra burst of energy. Without it, creative ideas are lost and never brought through to completion.

The circumstances of the final stage of a pregnancy are very important in the development of this ability to follow through efficiently. If the mother's energy was too low at this point and this slowed the last stage of the baby's growth, or, if the labour was weak, the child will develop into the kind of person who has many ideas, but never actually finishes anything.

Rowan is often used in magical workings to give that

required impulse to ambitions and desires. Rowan's greater use is in healing where it can be used to build this important quality into the psyche.

Ash

Ash is related to inspiration and intuition. The tree is associated with the expansion of the pituitary gland in the mother during pregnancy and breast feeding. Although this period overlaps in time with the early phases of growth associated with the Rowan and the Alder, a different emphasis is brought in by the energies of the Ash.

During this time of pituitary activity, a woman's intuition is at its highest. It is important for the developing child to feel the effect of its mother's intuition, since from her it will learn to trust in the tides of lunar energy that nourish and nurture its astral body and develop its psychic abilities. At this time, a mother needs to use her intuition to prepare for birth, to welcome the new soul and look after its individual needs. Too often at this moment the medical system takes control; the mother loses trust in herself and gives up her power to the doctors. The result is that the baby is brought through in a safe, clinical way that does not respect its emotional, psychic or spiritual needs. If this is the case the child does not learn to trust in its mother's intuitive knowledge, or in her ability to look after and nurture it. Consequently, it does not learn to trust in the wisdom and nourishment of Nature. The child then will grow up limited by the shortsightedness so often associated with being human, out of touch with its deeper nature, continuously giving away power to authority.

Ash is very much a lunar tree, but considered to be male. It provides the courage and dynamism to listen to your own intuition, to trust and act on your own innate knowledge, in spite of society's pressure to conform. It enables you to take back power and open up your life to encompass spiritual matters. It develops trust in Nature, the great Mother who looks after our needs on all levels. It is a tree that is both male and female, and relates to both parents. Although, at the time of birth, the mother is the more intuitive of the parents, she is also the more vulnerable, and the father is needed here to stand up for her and help her to deal with the birth in the way she knows is right. If either of the parents failed in their function at this time, Ash can provide the missing quality to their child. It is capable of both opening a person to intuition and providing the strength needed to follow its prompting.

Alder

Alder is the tree of birth. Traditionally it is the haunt of fairies, and both good and bad spirits have been known to live in it. It is related to birth in that it is a doorway into this world, but it does not discriminate: it can bring through both positive and negative energies. Therefore, discrimination is needed when one works with Alder. The quality of one's discrimination depends very much on one's experience at the moment of birth. At birth, a baby depends on its mother for help to push through into the world. If the birth is not natural, and the baby does not feel its mother's support, it no longer knows what to trust in, so insecurity and confusion result. As the child grows up, it will not be able to discriminate clearly between what can support it and what is hurtful. Birth is both painful and beautiful, in the same way that light and dark can be said to be two sides of the same coin. This is the lesson taught by the Alder. It is our non-acceptance of this fact that causes us to either let in harmful experiences, or to shy away from things that may end up being of great benefit.

The insecurity resulting from this lack of trust is stored in the psoas muscle, which has an important role during childbirth. In a woman who is holding on to her own birth trauma the effectiveness of this muscle may be reduced and she could find that the delivery is as difficult for her as it was for her mother.

Alder helps us to encompass light and dark, and by finding balance, to gain clear and accurate discrimination through all the difficult challenges and decisions that life can bring. It corresponds in the human psyche with birth and the first few weeks of life, when a baby is at its most dependent and clings to its mother. For those many people who find they always seek guidance outside themselves when they have to take a decision, looking for difficulties in this early stage of their life may provide the reason.

Willow

Willow is the tree of dreaming; its time of year is the early spring, when life is new and fresh. The ability to dream marks a very important stage in the development of the young child. A child learns to dream before it learns to think and before it is aware of responsibility. It is a time of simple trust when a child does not need to consider the consequences of its actions, or what its needs are. If a child did not dream, its life would be quite robotic and purposeless, dominated by logical actions and responsibilities. Dreaming develops first, before thought, because it tells us more about our correct purpose in life. Without knowledge of that purpose there is no fulfilment in life. When we dream we develop imagination, desire and personal goals, and keep a sense of the other realities that lie beyond the material world.

Dreams also help in self-healing and creating emotional balance, because they provide a way of releasing many tensions from the unconscious. If a child is disturbed at this stage of its development and loses touch with the dream world, its later life will be dull and lacking in purpose, with lowered vitality and a susceptibility to disease. The brain hemispheres will not be perfectly balanced which can cause dyslexia.

If you lose touch with your dreams you can become aware

of them again by sleeping with a Willow wand under your pillow. From the first your dreams will become more vivid and meaningful and then, later, the effect will filter through into waking life. Desire and vitality will be restored, together with a renewed sense of purpose and the will to live.

Whitethorn

Whitethorn is the tree of the awakening that follows the dream state. Its time of year is after the spring equinox, when life is really waking up; birds and animals begin their nest building and start to generally take care of their future.

This is the time that a young child, growing towards adolescence, begins to be aware of the 'real' world. The child knows that it is going to have to be responsible and, therefore, feels vulnerable. It is at this time that a child learns to be a victim, because it is then at its most helpless. A child needs encouragement if it is to gradually learn to cope with increasing responsibility and demands. If it is pushed too much, a child will dig in its heels and refuse to grow up. This is the mechanism which results in the adult 'victim' personality. Such an individual will be prone to all kinds of victimization, never able to handle all the difficulties that life may throw at him or her.

Whitethorn is one of the protective trees used, traditionally, to make psychic shields, particularly for the innocent and vulnerable. It can be given to a child to protect it from any harsh energies in the environment. Often a child is most open to psychic phenomena around puberty, and a Whitethorn tree spirit is extremely valuable to protect it at this sensitive time. Whitethorn's other use in healing is to resolve the victim complex that keeps an individual vulnerable. Whitethorn will heal the 'inner child', and build the courage needed to take on the normal tasks, problems and responsibilities of adult life.

Oak

Oak is the tree of strength. It relates to the stage of a young adult at the peak of vitality. At this time will and self-determination are at their strongest. The young person will have mastered the trials of adolescence, perhaps completed his or her education, and now feels confident and at ease, ready to build a life. Pride comes before a fall, however, and the over confident youth may realise that life is not necessarily easy from here on, and consequently feel let down and disappointed.

The Oak tree accumulates patience and great wisdom as it grows slowly into a giant. It can lend that patience and wisdom to those who, like the youth, want to gain everything too soon. Its energies can help to build our life's work gradually. It restores the will and self-determination that may be lost through disappointment, and restores faith in what we are working towards. The tree balances will at its strongest with patience. The Oak tree develops strength of character based on a simple faith in who we are and what we are to become. Everything we do depends upon faith. Without faith we would not be able to take our first step and learn to walk. Faith has been defined as the assurance of things hoped for. With faith we go ahead and achieve all our goals. Whenever faith is lost through disappointment or it is undermined by others, Oak can restore it.

Faith is most needed and most tested when a young adult leaves home to build his own life. If he fails and has no faith to start again, the liver is weakened. Oak can be used to heal this condition and release all patterns of failure.

Holly

Holly is the tree of sacrifice. At one time the Holly King was sacrificed each year to symbolise the male ego giving way to feminine power. The Holly represents the stage of the adult who having achieved everything for himself, lets go of his selfish path and considers others, taking on the feminine qualities of giving and nurturing. Going beyond selfishness is the first step to opening to forces beyond oneself, and thereby to the opening of intuition (another 'feminine' quality) and to a deeper spiritual life which brings fulfilment.

By this stage many personal desires may have had to be 'sacrificed' in order to raise a family. True sacrifice, however, does not involve giving up self for others. It is the sacrifice of a lower ideal for a higher one. Although life has taught you to have a less selfish attitude and you consider others when making decisions, at this stage of spiritual development you have new ideals to live by, and must not lose your path. The danger here is that you lose sight of your purpose and merely become a slave to the wishes of others in your family or group. Slavery is never rooted in love. Holly brings love and compassion and opens you to another lesson - the understanding of pain. Opening your heart can often open you to deeper pain. Often we accept suffering to shield those we love from pain. Holly reminds us that all beings feel pain as they grow and it is not our responsibility to keep them from this pain. Our love can help people, but it should not keep them from their pain. Without this understanding we are prone to emotional vampirism. It is important to learn this lesson and to apply it in one's healing practice as well as in the home. Many patients will want to unload their problems on to you, and you need to remember the difference between sympathy and compassion. Through love you can teach others to deal with their own pain.

Holly is commonly used to cut emotional ties and aka cords which have been formed by draining relationships. It should also be used in meditation to help you gain a balanced understanding of compassion and pain, so that you learn not to be drained in the future.

Hazel

Hazel is the tree of feminine power. It brings you psychic abilities as well as nurturing and healing energies, and a caring nature. It relates to the stage of human existence characterised by a mother with her children. When a mother is breast feeding, the pituitary gland (related to psychic ability) is stimulated, and oxytocin production is also increased (enhancing giving, nurturing qualities, and tolerance), thus psychic ability and a giving heart can come together. Hazel teaches us the importance of the heart, rather than the mind or the will. It also bears the most flexible wood which bends far without snapping. Hazel twigs are used traditionally for dowsing. When the process of giving birth and raising young children is interfered with by the medical profession and a woman gives away her power, not only does the child suffer but the woman is robbed of her intuition and the healing power that would develop naturally at this time. This applies equally to men in their process of 'giving birth' to new ideas and projects, which can also be limited by authorities. Hazel attunes to the Moon, which feeds our souls, awakens our desires and visions, and strengthens our astral bodies, making us more tolerant and resilient. It is a very important tree because it gives us the lunar energy which is so much denied in our patriarchal society. Without lunar energy we have no inner vision, and lack the still centre that can keep us stable in a stressful environment.

Hazel has many healing uses because it can restore our power and authority when these have been taken away by society, build up our vital energy, calm our nerves, and restore our intuition and connectedness to Nature.

Apple

Apple is the tree of abundance. Its moon is in the harvest season, when we reap the abundance that Nature produces so freely. At this time Nature gives all it has, in total trust that all will be replenished the next year. Giving freely is a part of its life cycle; without this activity no-one would survive. Whilst everything else gives all it has, mankind alone holds back, out of greed and insecurity, The apple tree has no need to hold on to any of its fruit because each new crop will be larger than that of the previous year. The fruit is given freely to those that need it, in recognition of their importance in the greater scheme of things. When we hold back we close our hearts and begin to die. With a closed heart we cannot experience oneness with life, our energy declines and our problems overwhelm us. Those people in life who give the most become indispensable, and are always looked after in the end. Those who only receive are not needed by anyone, so their insecurity gets greater and greater. Either way, the pattern is perpetuated. Apple teaches us that our true power is built up by giving, not receiving. By giving we open up to a new flow. By giving love and energy in addition to giving on a material level we are recognising that there is a limitless supply. We will not get in touch with that supply if we do not use it and demonstrate our trust in it by giving. Apples are a natural remedy for the stomach, bowels and heart, the main organs of giving and receiving. The tree spirit can be used to heal those who harm themselves with their miserliness; it can help all of us to keep our trust in times of lack.

Blackthorn

Blackthorn is the tree of the dragon, the guardian of Earth's treasures. Its blackness represents the void, the source we reach towards as we grow spiritually, and the thorns represent the pain we go through to get there. Blackthorn is another protective tree. Whereas Whitethorn protects the innocent, Blackthorn's protection is for the person who has built up his life and is subject to the jealousy of others. Like opposing a dragon, if you try to steal from or otherwise abuse that which Blackthorn protects, you will come up against a powerful force. The dragon is very much a symbol of those unconscious forces, fears and limitations, which we must face in ourselves if we are to obtain power. Once you have worked through all the fear, pain and resistance, this force becomes your friend and protector. This is why the dragon has been portrayed as both guardian and terrifying monster.

The Blackthorn tree spirit is used as a psychic shield. It is used also as a healer and initiator, because it helps you to face all the pain that you are carrying. The transmutation of pain through love is marked by the rising of the Kundalini, which is akin to dragon fire. Basically, Blackthorn's function is as a protector, not only to protect you from others, but to guard the power until you are wise enough to use it.

Elder

Elder is the tree of wisdom. This is the wisdom we must obtain before the Blackthorn gives us power, the wisdom to love everything and everybody without judgement. Wisdom is usually associated with maturity. The white flowers, followed by red berries and then by black berries are symbolic of a maturing process which takes a human through the stages of maiden, mother and crone. When you meditate with the Elder tree you may feel as if you are not quite evolved enough to really listen to its teachings. Do not let this put you off, it will always feel that way, no matter how much you grow, because the Elder always reminds us that we have further to go. We can never know everything, and because of this, we have no right to judge anything.

Elder also shows us that everything has its opposite, and both sides are equally important in the greater scheme. With this realisation we never judge anything. When we have no judgement towards other beings, we are then responsible enough to be given power. Power would be dangerous in the hands of a judgemental person. With judgement not only do we restrict others, we also limit ourselves and wear ourselves down. Judgement is very draining, because it closes down the contact with the limitless source and causes us to spend a great deal of energy in the protection of a false belief. Elder flower tea is a great remedy for tiredness and nervous exhaustion.

The Elder tree spirit helps us grow beyond judgement, brings us above dualities, and, therefore, allows us to open to limitless energy.

Yew

Yew is the tree of death and represents access to that other world. It is traditionally planted in graveyards to help the spirits of the dead cross the threshold. It reminds us that there is much beyond the material plane, and helps us to see beyond the illusion of mortality. It also helps us to overcome our fear of death, and by freeing ourselves from that fear, to find a great stillness within. As we gain the ability to see beyond the material plane, our material life becomes less important to us and we are more able to handle traumas linked to it. When we make something too 'real' we are unable to change it. If we think that the material life is all there is, we cannot bear anything that threatens it. By realising that there are other levels of existence that are more important, and by understanding the illusionary nature of the life that we have ourselves created, we can find a way to handle our worst traumas.

The knowledge that the Yew brings us makes it an extremely important tree for healing. It has been said, by some traditional sources, that of all the tree spirits Yew should not be used for healing, because of its association with death, but this is only because many people lack self-responsibility. Yew does not take our problems from us, it gives us insight to grow through them. The healing wands I use the most are Yew. The Yew also teaches us how to make changes in our material lives, and how to work towards our goals. By making things less 'real', we are more able to change them.

Although Yew is the last tree in the cycle, it symbolises rebirth, and the beginning of the cycle anew. Whether we are entering the physical plane or a new plane of existence, it is a kind of rebirth which follows seeing beyond our limitations.

APPENDIX - ADDITIONAL INFORMATION

Habundia Flower Essences

Flower essences have been used since the time of Ancient Egypt. Their full power has only been partly rediscovered in the 20th century. Imhotep wrote of using "earthly plant essences" to form a union of body and mind and spirit, and thus prepare the present for the future. The Egyptian magicians knew the subtle power that could be invoked by deep communion with the flower devas and were able to invoke their full co-operation to prepare elixirs which would have profound effects. Flower essences taken without the full conscious co-operation of the deva are but pale reflections of the power of these essences.

Habundia Flower Essences are prepared in the traditional sacred manner, by sensitive healers in deep communion with the devas. We only take those flowers which are freely given with purpose. The preparation of a flower essence may take many days, depending on how the energy of the individual flower wants to be worked. Furthermore, we only use fresh spring water drawn from holy wells, or fresh dew collected before dawn. Using these essences gives the possibility of attuning with the full power of the deva.

To obtain a catalogue of the Flower Essences or to arrange for a personal consultation with a practising healer please contact:

Habundia Flower Essences
PO BOX 90,
TOTNES, DEVON TQ11 0YG

Workshops in these arts are held also from time to time. Details can be obtained from the same address.

About the Author

Peter Aziz was born in London in 1960, into a family with a deep shamanic blood-line. His maternal grandmother was from a long line of Hungarian Shamans. Peter started practising yoga at the age of eight and at that time realised he had a communication with nature spirits that others seemed to lack. His deceased Grandmother often came in vision to teach him. During these years of childhood and adolescence he spent much of his time alone under trees.

In 1981 he obtained his BSc in Physics at Bedford College, London and two years later his calling to a spiritual focus led to a move to the West Country. At this time he withdrew into the forest alone for two months in order to seek vision. He then decided to move to Glastonbury, Somerset and practise Shamanic Healing. He studied Acupuncture, Kinesiology and Homeopathy as a foundation and then travelled to the United States several times to learn new shamanic healing methods. In 1987 he went to the Hawaiian island of Maui to study Body Electronics, and here he met Kahuna teachers, who taught him further shamanic principles. On returning home he withdrew into the wilderness once more, for four months, to absorb and integrate all he had learned and to receive further vision. During this period he evolved his current system of healing. He practises as a healer, and runs seminars to teach shamanic healing to others. He married in 1989, and now has a daughter and a son.

Peter Aziz' reputation as a remarkable healer is beginning to catch the attention of both the local and national press. In a recent article about the seemingly impossible recovery of her four-year-old son, left largely paralysed after a freak fit, his mother said "I took Calvin to see a homeopath when the doctors said they could do nothing more for him. He (*Peter Aziz*) has given him natural remedies, acupressure and spiritual healing.....Now Calvin can pull himself up to standing, and his speech is improving by the minute. I believe one day soon he will be able to walk".

Peter's response was, as ever, unassuming " I am simply working with nature's own remedies - you would be surprised what can happen!"

Shamanic Healing Courses

If you would like to find out more about the one-year Shamanic Healing course and other shorter Body Electronics workshops and courses please write for details to:

Peter Aziz
PO BOX 90,
TOTNES,
DEVON TQ11 0YG